FAN FARE

FAN FARE ★

A Playbook of *Great Recipes* for TAILGATING or Watching the Game at *Home*

DEBBIE MOOSE

The Harvard Common Press ■ Boston, Massachusetts

The Harvard Common Press
535 Albany Street
Boston, Massachusetts 02118
www.harvardcommonpress.com

Printed in the United States of America
Printed on acid-free paper

Library of Congress Cataloging-in-Publication Data
Moose, Debbie.
   Fan fare : a playbook of great recipes for tailgating or watching the game at home / Debbie
Moose.
       p. cm.
   Includes index.
   ISBN 978-1-55832-338-4 (hardcover : alk. paper)
   1. Outdoor cookery. 2. Tailgate parties. 3. Sports spectators. I. Title.
   TX823.M6568 2007
   641.5'78—dc22

                                                                              2007002509

Special bulk-order discounts are available on this and other Harvard Common Press books.
Companies and organizations may purchase books for premiums or resale, or may arrange a
custom edition, by contacting the Marketing Director at the address above.

Cover recipe: Double Play Spicy Beef, page 88
Back cover recipes, from left to right: Smoky Quesadillas, page 25; Munchable Marinated
Shrimp, page 28; and Jo Ann's Foiled Chicken Poppers, page 22

Cover design by Night & Day Design
Interior design by Richard Oriolo
Cover photographs by Joyce Oudkerk Pool
Food styling by Dan Becker; prop styling by Tabletop Props
For additional photo credits, see page 163

10 9 8 7 6 5 4 3 2 1

*For Rob,
the reason why my skies are
always Carolina blue*

Acknowledgments

Most importantly, thanks to all the food-loving sports fans who shared their recipes and stories for this book. And a big thanks goes to my colleagues in the Association of Food Journalists for advice and some great sources.

A team of intrepid tasters stepped up to the plate to help evaluate the recipes: Martha Waggoner; Art Eisenstadt; Mo and Bobbi Courie; Martha Abernethy; Sue Wilson; Jean Alderman; Gary and Judy Ogle; Kathy Wilson; Bill and Treva Jones (Treva, you pack the bolt cutters on our next trip); the Literary Lovelies; everyone who has come to our jambalaya Christmas parties over the years; all the UNC fans who have attended our Atlantic Coast Conference Tournament brunches, even when the Heels weren't playing (hey, the food was still good); Tom Attaway; Chuck Small; my husband's coworkers; the Avent West MOB (Minds on Books book club); the Elan Group; and the Brookhill Steeplechase gang.

I owe big thanks to Anne Saker for her advice and support and to Ruth Sheehan for her "brat" expertise. Also, thank you to Arturo Ciompi for wine suggestions. Finally, a huge thanks goes to WSHA-FM in Raleigh for playing the best jazz soundtrack for writing a cookbook.

For their inspiration, I'd like to offer special thanks to UNC basketball coach Roy Williams (Go Heels!) and to Duke basketball coach Mike Krzyzewski, because every epic struggle needs a good villain in addition to a great hero.

Finally, thanks go to my agent, Carla Glasser, with the Betsy Nolan Literary Agency, for her support and guidance throughout my literary journey.

Contents

Introduction   xi

STRATEGY SESSION *Proper Prior Planning*   1

KICKOFF *Snacks, Appetizers, and Drinks*   10

BOWL GAMES *Soups, Beans, and Chili*   44

HOT STREAK *Main Courses*   68

PIT STOPS *Salads, Sides, Breakfast, and Brunch*   106

OVERTIME *Desserts*   134

Game Plans: Menus for Every Occasion   147
Measurement Equivalents   149
Index   151

Introduction

As all fervent sports fans know, the day truly is won or lost in the tailgate.

Stats mean nothing—the sauce is everything.

The grilling game rules.

And extra points mean dessert.

Unlike on the field or track, everyone can be a winner during the tailgate, where hope rises like the aroma of grilling chicken. The superstitious may insist on the presence of certain talismans—a lucky team hat, for example, or the potato salad that a friend brought to the last winning tilt. We all know that those offerings influence the gods of sport. And they taste good—in the case of the potato salad, at least.

While all tailgaters share passion for their teams, how they express that passion in food has different flavors in different parts of the country. In Hawaii, fans of the University of Hawaii Warriors bring hibachis to grill fish from the waters around the islands, often caught by the fans themselves. Southerners take food and football seriously. In Raleigh, North Carolina, one dedicated fan of the North Carolina State University Wolfpack grills a chicken feast with his special family sauce for more than 50 hungry supporters. And in Wisconsin, hardy followers of the Green Bay Packers fuel up with grilled bratwurst and all the trimmings before battles on the frozen tundra of Lambeau Field.

Football games are the classic tailgate sites, but fans of other sports have to fuel up, too. Those who love the speed of NASCAR racing enjoy several days to a week of prerace feasting while camping with other fans. Even the mushers of the Iditarod Trail Sled Dog Race in Alaska partake of hearty fare along their chilly route.

Watching games at home requires the right kind of food, too. In addition, libations can flow more liberally there, in the absence of parking lot or campus restrictions.

Tailgate can be a noun or a verb, the result of impromptu inspiration or weeks of planning, outdoors or in the living room. But it always means good eating.

Proper Prior Planning

For me, the link between fans and food all started with a *sausage ball*.

In my first job, working at a small North Carolina newspaper, my apartment was a five-minute drive away. One fateful Friday, the first round of the annual Atlantic Coast Conference Basketball Tournament loomed. We University of North Carolina at Chapel

Hill fans realized that we could get to my place and see a good hour of the game (the managing editor being lenient) on our lunch break. This was before newsrooms were festooned with TVs, so there was no watching in the office.

Being a good Southern girl, I felt obligated to offer my guests some refreshment, but I wasn't much of a cook back then. I did make a mean sausage ball, though, and they were easy, plus meaty enough for the big-eating group.

I warmed the sausage balls and we dug in. Suddenly, a call went against our boys in baby blue. Enraged, a fellow reporter, whose name the annals record as Bill Moss, expressed his displeasure with the closest thing at hand. He flung a sausage ball at the TV screen, following it with speculation on the referee's parentage.

It was a moment that went down in sports food history. For me, after that day, food and sports were inexorably tied together. And each October, as college basketball season begins, I still stock an ample supply of sausage balls in my freezer. You just never know when some blind ref will make an idiot call.

Planning Ahead

A great game plan is to do whatever you can ahead of time, so that when you get to the stadium or track (or when it's game time at home), all you have to do is have fun. The recipes in this book that are great for preparing the day before are noted, along with transportation tips. Here are some other timesaving suggestions for getting the food ready for the big event.

- ☛ Shape hamburger patties at home, stack them between pieces of waxed paper, and seal in zipper-top plastic bags.
- ☛ Store the filling for deviled eggs in a zipper-top plastic bag, then snip a small hole in the bottom and fill the eggs when you get to the tailgate.
- ☛ If you plan to cook with onions, garlic, carrots, celery, bell peppers, summer squash, hot peppers, etc., you can chop or slice them the night before and refrigerate them in separate zipper-top plastic bags.
- ☛ Wash salad greens or fresh herbs the night before, dry completely, and store them in zipper-top plastic bags.

What to Bring

The best tailgaters, like the best teams, are organized and prepared. Here's a basic checklist of items to take along when you're going "on location," most of which can be packed ahead of time. Serious fans keep a plastic tub packed with necessary nonperishables in the car for the entire season, replenishing supplies as needed.

- **Plates, bowls, cups, napkins, tablecloths, forks, spoons, and knives:** Some tailgaters use inexpensive, reusable plastic dinnerware and cloth tablecloths and napkins, not just for their looks, but because doing so can save money over time and cut down on trash. If you don't like washing up afterward, though, stick with disposables.
- **Several large trash bags:** Besides being used for trash, they can hold ice for serving chilled food or be used to cover food and gear in case of rain. You can't have too many of these on hand.
- **Disposable latex or rubber gloves:** These come in handy for handling raw meats and working with chile peppers.
- **Aluminum foil:** Use this to help keep food warm and bug-free and to cover grill grates for easy cleanup.
- **Zipper-top plastic bags:** Bring various sizes along for storing leftover food.
- **Disposable foil pans:** You can use these for so many things, such as holding food prior to grilling, serving cooked food, or making an ice bed to help keep food cold. Bring along several in various sizes.
- **Knives and plastic cutting boards:** Tape sharp knives between two pieces of cardboard to prevent accidental cuts in transit. If you're preparing raw meats on site, bring along color-coded cutting boards to avoid contamination of other foods (a red board for meat and a green board for veggies, for example).
- **Coolers:** Bring separate, labeled coolers for raw foods, cooked foods, beverages, and ice for drinks.
- **Thermoses:** They keep cold drinks cold and hot drinks (and soups) hot.
- **Ice:** This keeps both food and drinks cold. Bring along plenty of ice, particularly in warmer weather.
- **Can opener, bottle opener, and corkscrew:** The can opener is for food, the bottle opener and corkscrew for beer and wine, if alcohol is allowed at the tailgate site and if you plan to drink it.
- **Serving spoons and forks:** Bring sturdy, reusable plastic or wooden serving utensils.

- ☞ Flashlights or battery-powered lanterns: These will come in handy for evening festivities.
- ☞ Folding chairs and tables: Not everyone likes to eat standing up.
- ☞ A roll or two of paper towels: You'll be surprised how quickly you go through these.
- ☞ Disinfectant wipes and hand sanitizer: Use wipes for cleanup jobs and for cleaning your hands after eating messy food, and use hand sanitizer for quick cleanups after handling uncooked food.
- ☞ A gallon or two of water labeled for cleanup use: Fill plastic jugs from the tap at home.
- ☞ Dishwashing liquid: Use this for wiping down surfaces and cleaning your hands.
- ☞ Small first-aid kit: Include such items as adhesive bandages, antibacterial cream for cuts, insect repellent, medication for insect bites and burns, and sunscreen.
- ☞ Optional items: These might include a canopy for shade or rain protection and tarps for providing a mud- and dirt-free seating area. Look for both in your favorite team or driver colors. There are scores of other fun tailgating accessories, from everyday to high-end, to be found at numerous online sites; spend some time browsing if you are so inclined.

Grillers should add:
- ☞ The grill: Don't laugh. People have forgotten it.
- ☞ Hardwood charcoal or a propane gas canister: Again, don't laugh.
- ☞ Lighter or matches and charcoal chimney starter: You will need these if using a charcoal grill.
- ☞ Small wrench and screwdriver: Wouldn't you know it, suddenly the gas connections need adjusting.
- ☞ Instant-read thermometer: This helps ensure the safety of meat cooked on site.
- ☞ A couple of pairs of long-handled spring-loaded tongs and a long-handled spatula: These are for turning food while it cooks.
- ☞ Perforated grill pan or a grill basket: These prevent small or fragile items, such as vegetables and seafood, from falling through the grill grates.
- ☞ Oven mitts: Take two along for handling hot items.

Start Your Engines

Grilling is the top cooking method in the parking lot—just follow your nose for verification. Here are some brief tips on how to get excellent results from your preferred grilling technique.

Quick-cooking meats like pork chops and tenderloins, marinated boneless chicken breasts and steaks, burgers and hot dogs, and seafood are cooked over direct heat. Charcoal fans, that means placing the hot coals in the center of the grill; gas lovers, set your grills for direct cooking.

Longer-cooking items, such as whole chickens, call for indirect heat. Charcoalers, you pile coals on each side of the grill, leaving the center open; gas folks, just hit the indirect heat setting or, on an older grill, light the side burners, not the center one. If using charcoal, you'll need a charcoal chimney starter to start and replenish the coals as the cooking goes along. A charcoal chimney starter is simply a metal cylinder with a handle, an inexpensive gadget available at home-improvement stores, grilling stores, and even large grocery stores. You put coal in the top and stuff newspaper in the bottom, which you light to ignite the charcoal. The charcoal is usually ready in about 30 minutes. Do not place a chimney starter on grass when lighting it; use it on concrete, asphalt, or gravel. The chimney will get very hot, so keep children away and use an oven mitt when moving it to pour the lighted charcoal into the grill.

Definitely use hardwood lump charcoal and go the charcoal chimney route or use solid starters made from paraffin. One paraffin starter, nestled in the charcoal, should start a small portable grill; use two for a regular-sized one. Carrying lighter fluid around can be dangerous, and besides, it makes the food taste like gasoline. The quick-starting brands of briquettes are permeated with lighter fluid and have the same smell and flavor problem. Also, they don't stay hot for very long.

As much fun as grilling is, you are handling fire, so take some precautions. Place the grill on firm, level ground, away from anything flammable, such as grass, trees, or shrubs (that includes your car). If you're concerned about the area you have to use—tailgaters can't always be choosers—cover the surface under the grill and a radius of a couple of feet surrounding the grill with heavy-duty aluminum foil before starting. Keep small children back from the fire, and don't wear clothing with loose sleeves. Make sure the grill is away from the rest of the tailgate action, so that guests won't bump into it.

When the cooking is done, do not pack up the grill until it is *completely* cool. Do not remove the charcoal and dispose of it until it is cold. The hot action should stay on the field, not end up in the trunk of your car or a parking lot dumpster.

The Obligatory Food Safety Lecture

Yes, sports fans, there are things worse than being slapped with a 15-yard penalty with goal to go, collecting that final foul, or getting black-flagged on the last lap. Ignoring food safety can put a damper on the party faster than you can ask, "Where's the nearest emergency room?"

Basically, the idea is to keep cold things cold and hot things hot. But when you're tailgating outdoors, especially in warm weather, that takes a little work. Even indoors, food safety is important. You need to be aware of how long food has been sitting out at room temperature and remove it from the serving area if you feel it might have been out too long.

Thoroughly chill any cold items, such as salads, dips, or drinks, before packing them in the cooler for traveling. If you're taking raw meat or seafood to grill on site, put it in leakproof zipper-top plastic bags or airtight containers, and pack it deep into the center of the cooler, which is the coldest part. Use plenty of ice. You want the food to stay really cold, and the ice will melt as time goes on, even in a cooler. Also, never consume ice that may have come into contact with raw meat. Label a separate, clean cooler of ice solely for beverage use. And remember: If you run out of ice, no one has yet expired from drinking a warm soda, but a foodborne illness can slap you down harder than a 300-pound linebacker. Don't take the risk. Besides, you don't want to miss the game.

Cleanliness is as important as temperature when handling raw meats or eggs. Carry along a jug of water and liquid soap just for hand-washing purposes. Disposable rubber or latex gloves are also useful for handling raw meats or fish. Hand sanitizer or antibacterial wipes can be used for quick cleanups.

And watch for cross-contamination. Don't use cutting boards, plates, knives, or utensils that have touched raw meats or raw eggs for anything else—put them in a separate, labeled bag or move them to an area away from other tailgate foods. To make this easier, you may want to invest in different colors of plastic cutting boards for your tailgating. Also, you can find knives with color-coded handles, or you can put colored stickers on the handles.

Once that glorious spread is laid out for hungry fans, keep an eye on the clock. Dips; cheeses; cooked meat, seafood, or eggs; salads that use mayonnaise or other dairy products; and the like should not be left out on a warm day for more than two hours. Even at an indoor party, don't push the limit. Take out some insurance by nestling bowls of chilled items, such as cooked shrimp, into larger bowls or containers of ice for serving. Get fancy with bowls in your team colors, or go the easy way and put the ice in plastic tubs. There are also

Is It Done Yet?

Here are the correct internal temperatures for meat, poultry, and fish when taken with an instant-read thermometer inserted into the thickest part of the meat without touching bone.

BEEF ROASTS: 145°F for medium-rare, 160°F for medium. Stop cooking when the internal temperature is 5° to 10°F below the target, and let the meat stand for 15 to 20 minutes before carving, as the internal temperature will continue to rise.

BEEF STEAKS: 145°F for medium-rare, 160°F for medium

HAMBURGERS: 160°F for medium

PORK ROASTS, TENDERLOINS, AND CHOPS: 160°F

CHICKEN AND OTHER POULTRY: 180°F

FISH: Flakes with a fork inserted into the thickest part

SHELLFISH: Opaque throughout and firm when touched

numerous coolers, carriers, and food-chilling devices out there tailored specifically to tailgaters, made by several different manufacturers—invest in some of those, if you like.

To Beer or Not to Beer

As long as there have been tailgates, there has been drinking at tailgates. Serving and enjoying your favorite alcoholic beverages is a big part of hosting game-watching parties at home, too.

If you choose to imbibe at a tailgate, be sure to check the policy of the area where you're parking. Some colleges ban alcohol on campus property, and some family camping areas discourage drinking. Most places have rules about drinking, but some enforce them more strictly than others. We're all familiar with the use of the red plastic cup and the mystery of its contents. Just be sure you know what you're getting into if you choose to drink.

Here's the deal: If you're drinking, don't be stupid about it. Your team or favorite driver needs all fans healthy and whole to cheer them on to victory. The same goes if you're hosting a game-day event at home. Pocket the keys if a guest has overindulged. It's the right call.

Good Excuses for a Tailgate

Sports fans can find an excuse for a party—and for eating big—during any month of the year. Here are some handy reminders, so you never have to go too long without a tailgate.

JANUARY

College football bowl games
NFL playoffs

FEBRUARY

Super Bowl
Daytona 500
Winter Olympics (every four years)
NBA All-Star Game

MARCH

NCAA Basketball Championship
(March Madness)
Iditarod Trail Sled Dog Race
Cricket World Cup

APRIL

Masters Golf Tournament

MAY

Kentucky Derby
Indianapolis 500
NASCAR All-Star Challenge

JUNE

NBA playoffs
NHL championship
College World Series
U.S. Open golf tournament

JULY

World Cup soccer finals (every four years)
Wimbledon tennis tournament
Major League Baseball All-Star Game

AUGUST

Summer Olympics (every four years)
U.S. Open tennis tournament
(August–September)

SEPTEMBER

WNBA playoffs
College football season heats up

OCTOBER

Major League Baseball World Series
Rugby World Cup (every four years)

NOVEMBER

NASCAR Chase final race

DECEMBER

College football bowl games

Tailgate Fever

*I*n the beginning, there was food, followed quickly by sports. Exactly when the two came together is debated. Yale claims to be the site of the first pre-football tailgate in 1904, when fans arriving by train for a game brought picnics. However, Princeton and Rutgers make competing claims, saying that at their first football game in 1869, fans carried in food by carriage.

No matter who started the whole thing, tailgating has spread across our land like smoke from sizzling ribs. At the University of Washington in Seattle, fans sail right up to the stadium and tailgate in boats on Lake Washington, then go inside and enjoy one of the most gorgeous views from any football arena. The tailgate for the Georgia-Florida game in Jacksonville has grown so big that it has its own name: The World's Largest Outdoor Cocktail Party.

Fans of other sports like to eat, too. They can tailgate all night at the Midnight Sun, a baseball game played on the summer solstice each year in Fairbanks, Alaska. The game starts at 10:30 P.M. and goes on, without the need for artificial lighting, until around 2:00 A.M. Rowing regattas on the Charles River in Boston, Massachusetts, and polo matches in West Palm Beach, Florida, have their own tailgating styles. And NASCAR fans are a whole 'nother breed.

Don't forget those who bring the tailgate home, with lavish Super Bowl viewing parties, get-togethers for fight nights, or Kentucky Derby soirees. Some fans try to combine the best of the on-location and at-home worlds, as does one University of Tennessee supporter who hangs a sheet on the side of his house, sets up a projection TV, and brings the action and food home for dozens of friends.

After more than 100 years of tailgating, it still all comes down to three things: fans, food, and fun.

Snacks, Appetizers, and Drinks

These *munchies* will start your engines at any tailgate, and they'll keep the party going no matter how furious the action gets. How about some *savory* marinated shrimp for early-season football watching or bacon-wrapped, chicken-stuffed jalapeños cooked over a campfire before a stock car race? And is anyone *thirsty*? Special libations for all events are here, including versions of that tailgate classic, the Bloody Mary. Your guests will be *screaming* for more. But don't worry about the yelling—it's good practice for the game.

Goal-to-Go Guacamole	12	Jo Ann's Foiled Chicken Poppers	22	Thomas's Tennessee Cocktail	31
Summer Tomato Spread	13	Gobble 'Em Up Nachos	23	Satan's Whiskers	32
Steeplechase Spread	14	Lisa's Amazing Appetizer	24	Brookhill Iced Tea	33
Masterful PC, Southern Style	15	Smoky Quesadillas	25	Lynchburg Lemonade	35
Revved-Up Onion Dip	16	Nutty Blue Cheese Ball	26	Blue Lagoon	38
Alissa's Eight-Layer Dip	17	Marylynn's Okra Roll-Ups	27	Denise's Mimosas	39
Chip Shots	18	Munchable Marinated Shrimp	28	Eddie's Bloody Mary	40
Rachel and Opal's Cheese Straws	19	Jo Ann's Campfire Onion Blossoms	29	Whassup, Mary?	41
Rosemary-Garlic Pecans	20			Smokin' Mary	42
Sweet-Hot Nuts	21	Slam-Dunk Sausage Balls	30	Red-Hot Cider	43

Goal-to-Go Guacamole

Some like jalapeños in their guacamole, but I'm a fan of the hotter bite of *fresh serranos*. Add more to turn up the heat. To peel the tomato, dunk it in boiling water (use a slotted spoon) for a minute or less. Hold the tomato under cold running water to cool, then slip off the skin. MAKES ABOUT 2 CUPS

2 small, ripe Hass avocados

1 small tomato, peeled and chopped
  (about $1/2$ cup)

1 green serrano chile, seeded and finely chopped

$1^1/2$ teaspoons canned chopped green chiles,
  drained

2 cloves garlic, crushed or finely chopped

$1/3$ cup freshly squeezed lime juice

$1/4$ cup chopped fresh cilantro

Salt to taste

Tortilla chips for serving

1 Cut the avocados in half, remove the pits, and scoop out the flesh into a medium-size bowl. Mash coarsely. Stir in the tomato, serrano chile, green chiles, garlic, lime juice, and cilantro. Add salt.

2 Cover and keep cold until ready to serve. Serve with tortilla chips.

EXTRA POINTS You can make this on site or a few hours before the tailgate. Press plastic wrap directly onto the surface of the guacamole to prevent it from browning.

Summer Tomato Spread

Take advantage of summer tomatoes and *fresh basil* to make big batches of this jellied spread for winter game viewing. Freeze in one-cup containers or refrigerate the spread in clean glass jars. Serve this spread layered over a block of cream cheese, as a condiment on a cheese platter, or simply by itself with crackers. MAKES 5 CUPS

5 large very ripe tomatoes (about 2 pounds)
$1/4$ cup freshly squeezed lemon juice
4 tablespoons chopped fresh basil
2 cloves garlic, finely chopped

1 package powdered pectin for lower-sugar recipes
$1 1/4$ cups sugar

1   Peel the tomatoes (see headnote, page 12). Remove the cores and seeds and roughly chop the tomatoes. Place in a Dutch oven or a large pot and bring to a boil. Reduce the heat and simmer for 10 minutes.

2   Add the lemon juice, basil, and garlic. Mix the pectin with $1/4$ cup of the sugar, then stir into the tomato mixture. Return to a boil, stirring constantly to prevent sticking. When the mixture comes to a boil, stir in the remaining 1 cup sugar. Let boil vigorously for 1 minute, stirring constantly. Remove from the heat.

3   Let the mixture cool, then pour into clean glass jars and refrigerate or pour into freezer bags or plastic freezer containers in 1-cup servings and freeze. When ready to use, thaw if necessary and stir to recombine.

EXTRA POINTS Make and refrigerate this spread up to 3 weeks before your tailgate. It will keep frozen for up to 6 months.

Steeplechase Spread

I've become a big fan of avocados, and I made this spread to take to the Brookhill Steeplechase in Clayton, North Carolina. The combination of the *smooth creaminess* from the avocados and the tartness of the lemon is refreshing on a warm day. I've suggested serving this with crackers, but you can also make tea sandwiches by spreading it on thinly sliced bread and topping it with thin slices of tomato. SERVES 6

2 ripe Hass avocados
1/2 cup plain yogurt
3 teaspoons freshly squeezed lemon juice
2 teaspoons chopped fresh cilantro
1/2 teaspoon salt

Dash of garlic powder
Dash of onion powder
Freshly ground black pepper to taste
Water crackers for serving

1   Cut the avocados in half, remove the pits, and scoop out the flesh into a medium-size bowl. Mash well. Stir in the yogurt, 2 teaspoons of the lemon juice, the cilantro, salt, garlic powder, onion powder, and black pepper. Stir until the mixture is very smooth.

2   Sprinkle the top with the remaining 1 teaspoon of lemon juice to keep the avocado from browning. Cover and chill for several hours, or refrigerate overnight.

3   Stir before serving. Serve with crackers.

EXTRA POINTS You can make this the day before serving if you wish. Press a sheet of plastic wrap directly onto the surface of the spread to keep it from browning.

Masterful PC, Southern Style

Pimiento cheese sandwiches are a tradition at the Masters Golf Tournament in Augusta, Georgia. The Masters folks like to keep their recipe secret, but I have my own way of making this Southern classic: *chunky and garlicky.* For a fresher flavor, don't use prepared shredded cheese. I like to use the food grinder attachment on my stand mixer to grate the cheddar, but you can also use a box grater. If you prefer a smoother texture, add more mayo and shred the cheese more finely. Serve this with a bread of your choice or on crackers. SERVES 6 TO 8

1 pound sharp cheddar cheese
½ of a medium-size sweet onion, coarsely chopped
1 large clove garlic, cut into quarters
⅔ cup mayonnaise

1½ teaspoons Dijon mustard
One 4-ounce jar chopped pimientos, drained
Dash of cayenne pepper
Salt and freshly ground black pepper to taste

1 Shred or grate the cheese to a medium-chunky texture and place in a large bowl.

2 Put the onion and garlic through a food grinder or food processor and stir into the cheese. Stir in the mayonnaise, mustard, pimientos, and cayenne pepper. Add salt and pepper.

3 Cover the mixture tightly and refrigerate for at least 8 hours or overnight to let the flavors blend.

EXTRA POINTS **Prepare this spread up to 3 days ahead and refrigerate in an airtight container.**

Revved-Up Onion Dip

I took this dip to a party to watch the Daytona 500, and it got the green flag! It's my version of the classic onion dip, with *fresher flavors* and less salt. Add more horseradish if you're a fan of that flavor. It's great with potato chips, crackers, or celery and carrot sticks, and it is equally good as a spread on slices of French bread.   MAKES 2 CUPS

1 medium-size sweet onion, such as Vidalia, OSO Sweet, or Texas 1050
3 cloves garlic
1 sprig fresh thyme (optional)
1$^1/_2$ cups sour cream
$^1/_2$ teaspoon freshly ground black pepper

1$^1/_4$ teaspoons Worcestershire sauce
$^1/_4$ teaspoon dried thyme
$^1/_4$ teaspoon cayenne pepper
$^1/_4$ teaspoon Dijon mustard
$^1/_2$ teaspoon prepared horseradish
Salt to taste

1   Preheat the oven to 375°F. Spray a baking dish and a small sheet of aluminum foil with nonstick cooking spray.

2   Place the unpeeled onion in the baking dish. Place the unpeeled garlic cloves and the sprig of fresh thyme, if using, on the foil and wrap securely. Place in the baking dish. Bake for 1$^1/_2$ hours, or until the onion is tender when pierced with a knife. Cool the onion and garlic until you can handle them, then remove the papery outside skins.

3   In a food processor, finely chop the onion and garlic, but do not puree. Place the mixture in a sieve and drain the excess liquid by pressing down with a spoon. Place the drained mixture in a large bowl. (Be sure the mixture is at room temperature before continuing.)

4   Add the sour cream, black pepper, Worcestershire sauce, thyme, cayenne pepper, mustard, and horseradish; stir well to combine. Add salt.

5   Refrigerate the dip until chilled and the flavors have blended, at least 2 hours or overnight.

EXTRA POINTS The onion and garlic can be roasted and chopped the day before making the dip; just cool and refrigerate, but bring back to room temperature before continuing. You can assemble the dip at the tailgate if you prefer, but it actually tastes even better if made the day before serving.

Alissa's Eight-Layer Dip

Alissa Abel of Charlotte, North Carolina, a Carolina Panthers football fan, says that she and her sister, Naomi, both make versions of this dip for game day parties, so it's all in the family. "It's always the *first thing to go*," Alissa says.

SERVES 12

2 medium-ripe Hass avocados
1 teaspoon freshly squeezed lemon juice
1 cup sour cream
One 15.2-ounce can refried black beans
2 cups chopped iceberg lettuce

2 cups chopped fresh tomatoes
One 3.8-ounce can sliced black olives, drained
1½ cups shredded cheddar cheese
1 cup chopped green onions
Tortilla chips for serving

1   Peel and pit the avocados and roughly chop the flesh. Toss the avocados with the lemon juice in a medium-size bowl immediately after chopping to prevent browning; set aside.

2   Use a clear glass 8 x 11-inch or 9 x 13-inch baking dish to assemble the dip so that you can see the layers. Spread the sour cream on the bottom of the dish, followed by the refried beans, lettuce, tomatoes, black olives, cheddar cheese, and green onions. Top with the avocados.

3   Serve immediately with tortilla chips.

EXTRA POINTS You can chop the lettuce and green onions the night before the game and refrigerate in zipper-top plastic bags, then quickly assemble the entire dip at the tailgate or game party. Don't chop the avocado or tomato until right before assembling the dip, though. And don't forget to take along a lemon to squeeze over the chopped avocado.

Chip Shots

Put yourself in the driver's seat and make the kinds of snack chips you like, rather than relying on bags from the supermarket shelf. It's easy to *make your own* pita chips, and they'll have less salt and fat, too. Try using dried herbs and/or chili powder to make interesting flavors. **MAKES ABOUT 64 CHIPS**

4 whole pita bread rounds
Olive oil for brushing
2 teaspoons garlic powder

1 teaspoon onion powder
$1/2$ teaspoon salt

1   Preheat the oven to 400°F.

2   Gently pull or cut the pitas apart, separating them into single layers. Using a serrated knife, cut each pita layer like a pie, into 8 wedges. Place the wedges, rough side up, on a rimmed nonstick baking sheet. Brush the rough side of each wedge lightly with olive oil.

3   In a small bowl, combine the garlic powder, onion powder, and salt. Sprinkle each wedge with the mixture. Bake for 10 minutes, or until the wedges are light brown and crispy. Let cool completely, then store in an airtight container.

EXTRA POINTS You can make these up to 1 week ahead of time. Experiment with different flavors:

- Chili powder, onion powder, garlic powder, and salt
- Curry powder, cumin, and salt
- Mixed Italian herbs, lemon pepper, and salt
- Cayenne pepper, black pepper, and salt

Rachel and Opal's Cheese Straws

Every great Southern tailgate features delicate, *crunchy* cheese straws. Southern cooks have been known to come to blows over who gets Grandma's ancient cookie press, which is traditionally used to produce these goodies. If your grandmother didn't leave one behind, you can roll the dough into a log and cut rounds by hand. This recipe is from a *great* compilation of down-home recipes called *Hungry for Home* (Novello Festival Press, 2003) by Amy Rogers. Rachel Evans and Opal Wicker are two cooks who passed down the recipe to Ann Wicker, who gave it to Amy. MAKES 24 TO 30

1/2 pound extra-sharp cheddar cheese
2 cups all-purpose flour
3/4 cup (1 1/2 sticks) unsalted butter, melted

1/4 teaspoon red pepper flakes
1 1/2 teaspoons salt

1 Preheat the oven to 400°F.

2 Shred the cheese and place it in a large bowl. Add the flour, butter, red pepper flakes, and salt. Using a large spoon, work the dough until completely mixed.

3 Put the dough into a cookie press with the star tip attached. Press out 2-inch-long strips onto ungreased cookie sheets, leaving about 1/2 inch between them. Or roll the dough into a log about 2 inches in diameter, wrap in plastic wrap, chill until firm, and then slice into rounds 1/4 inch thick.

4 Bake for 8 to 10 minutes, until golden. Remove to wire racks to cool.

EXTRA POINTS **After you bake the straws, you can cool them completely and store them in an airtight container for up to 1 week.**

Rosemary-Garlic Pecans

You will grab these by the handful. The rosemary flavor is a *nice change* from typical roasted pecan recipes. They'd be good atop a salad, too. Feel free to substitute almonds if you want a change of pace. SERVES 8 TO 10

2 tablespoons unsalted butter
2 tablespoons chopped fresh rosemary leaves
1 teaspoon garlic powder

1/2 teaspoon salt
1/2 teaspoon freshly ground black pepper
2 cups pecan halves or whole almonds

1 Preheat the oven to 350°F.

2 Melt the butter in a small bowl in the microwave. Stir in the rosemary, garlic powder, salt, and black pepper. Place the pecans in a large bowl, then pour the butter mixture over the pecans and toss to coat the nuts thoroughly.

3 Spread the pecans in a single layer on a rimmed nonstick baking sheet (or coat a regular baking sheet with nonstick cooking spray). Bake for about 20 minutes, stirring 2 or 3 times, until the pecans are crisp and fragrant but not dark.

4 Let the nuts cool completely on the baking sheet, then store in an airtight container.

EXTRA POINTS You can make these up to 1 week ahead of time.

Sweet-Hot Nuts

Many sweet roasted pecans are too sweet for my taste. This recipe combines sweet and hot in a *perfect* blend. Because of the sugar, watch them carefully while cooking to make sure they don't burn. SERVES 8 TO 10

2 tablespoons unsalted butter
1 tablespoon ground cinnamon
1 teaspoon chili powder
1/2 teaspoon salt

1/4 teaspoon freshly ground black pepper
1 tablespoon light brown sugar
2 cups pecan halves

1 Preheat the oven to 350°F.

2 Melt the butter in a small bowl in the microwave. Stir in the cinnamon, chili powder, salt, black pepper, and brown sugar. Place the pecans in a large bowl, then pour the butter mixture over the pecans and toss to coat the nuts thoroughly.

3 Spread the pecans in a single layer on a rimmed nonstick baking sheet (or coat a regular baking sheet with nonstick cooking spray). Bake for about 20 minutes, stirring 2 or 3 times, until the pecans are crisp and fragrant but not dark.

4 Let the nuts cool completely on the baking sheet, then store in an airtight container.

EXTRA POINTS You can make these up to 1 week ahead of time.

Jo Ann's Foiled Chicken Poppers

Jo Ann Hlavac of Charleston is known as *Race Mama* to the devotees of www.laidbackracing.com. Jo Ann and her husband, Jimmy, have been traveling to NASCAR races for more than 20 years and have exhaustive information on each track on their Web site. Because Jo Ann and Jimmy camp in their RV for several days before a race, most of her favorite recipes, like this one, are cooked outdoors. MAKES 20 PIECES

10 large fresh jalapeño chiles
1 pound chicken tenders, cut to fit the
   jalapeños if necessary

1 pound bacon

1   Light a hot fire in a charcoal grill, or preheat a gas grill.

2   Cut the jalapeños in half lengthwise and remove the stems, seeds, and ribs.

3   Place 1 chicken tender in each jalapeño half. Wrap 1 slice of bacon around each stuffed jalapeño. Continue until all the jalapeño halves are stuffed and wrapped.

4   Place the stuffed chiles on a sheet of heavy-duty aluminum foil and wrap securely. Place the packet on the grill and cook for about 20 minutes, or until the chicken and bacon are done. Serve hot or warm.

EXTRA POINTS You can stuff, wrap, and refrigerate the poppers the day before the tailgate. Or, if you prefer to assemble them on site, carry frozen chicken tenders in a cooler to the tailgate, and they should be thawed and ready for cooking by the time you've settled in and fired up the grill.

Gobble 'Em Up Nachos

When I go to a basketball game, the radioactive-looking yellow nachos served at the concession stands always smell so good, but I know their flavor won't measure up. Why not make a winning version of nachos for game-watching at home? Using *ground turkey* makes these snacks lower in fat—but don't tell the fellas.   SERVES 6 TO 8

1 tablespoon vegetable oil
1 pound ground turkey
1 large onion, chopped
2 cloves garlic, chopped
Two 12-ounce jars chili sauce
1 tablespoon plus 1 teaspoon chili powder
2^1/$_2$ teaspoons dried oregano
1^1/$_4$ teaspoons ground cumin
^{1}/$_4$ teaspoon salt
One 2-ounce jar pimientos, drained
One 4-ounce can chopped green chiles

^{1}/$_2$ cup beer, such as a classic American lager
   (do not use a sweet ale)
1 tablespoon cider vinegar
Hot pepper sauce to taste (optional)
Freshly ground black pepper to taste
^{1}/$_2$ cup chopped fresh cilantro
One 12-ounce bag tortilla chips
1 cup shredded Mexican-blend, cheddar, or
   Monterey Jack cheese, or more to taste
^{1}/$_2$ cup sliced pickled jalapeño chiles, drained, or
   more to taste
Sour cream for garnish

1   Place the vegetable oil in a large nonstick frying pan over medium heat. When the oil is hot, add the turkey and onion. Stir and cook, breaking up the turkey, until it is almost cooked through. Add the garlic and continue to cook until the turkey is done.

2   Stir in the chili sauce, chili powder, oregano, cumin, salt, pimientos, green chiles, beer, vinegar, and hot pepper sauce, if using. Add black pepper. Cover, reduce the heat, and simmer for 5 minutes. Add the cilantro, cover, and simmer for an additional 5 minutes. If the mixture is too thick, add a little water. At this point, you can reduce the heat to low and keep warm, covered.

3   To serve, place the tortilla chips on a large serving platter. Pour the turkey mixture over the chips and immediately sprinkle on the cheese, allowing the heat from the mixture to melt the cheese. Sprinkle on the jalapeños. Offer the sour cream on the side.

EXTRA POINTS Prepare and refrigerate the turkey mixture the day before the tailgate. Reheat it in a heavy pan on the grill.

Lisa's Amazing Appetizer

Lisa West of Raleigh, North Carolina, serves this snack at parties of all kinds, and she says it's *always a hit*. Dedicated cooks may recognize this recipe as a twist on the French classic *brie en croûte*—but this version is easy, Southern style. SERVES 6 TO 8

One 8-ounce package refrigerated crescent rolls
One 8-ounce package cream cheese
1 large egg, beaten

Crackers for serving
Hot pepper relish for serving

1 Preheat the oven to 350°F.

2 Remove the crescent roll dough from the package and gently press it out into a rectangle, sealing any perforations. Place the whole block of cream cheese in the center of the dough. Pull the sides of the dough up to completely cover the cream cheese. Press the dough firmly to seal, being careful not to tear the dough.

3 Place the wrapped cheese on a nonstick cookie sheet. Brush the top and sides with the beaten egg. Bake for about 15 minutes, or until the dough is browned.

4 Place on a platter and serve warm surrounded by crackers, with hot pepper relish in a small bowl on the side.

EXTRA POINTS This is best served immediately after baking.

Smoky Quesadillas

Smoked cheeses lend a deep flavor to quesadillas. I got the idea for this snack after sampling some *wonderful* smoked fresh mozzarella from a local cheesemaker, but smoked Gouda will offer great flavor as well. SERVES 8 TO 10

One 15-ounce can black beans, rinsed and drained

One 4-ounce can chopped green chiles

1/4 cup chopped green onions

1/2 teaspoon chili powder

1 cup chopped smoked fresh mozzarella cheese or shredded smoked Gouda cheese

8 to 10 large flour tortillas

Sour cream for serving

Salsa for serving

1   Combine the black beans, chiles, green onions, chili powder, and cheese in a large bowl. Stir well.

2   Place a tortilla on a clean work surface. Place about 1/3 cup of the filling on one half of the tortilla, spreading the filling to the edges. Fold the other half of the tortilla over the filling. Continue with the remaining tortillas.

3   Spray a large nonstick skillet with cooking spray and place over medium heat. Place 2 quesadillas in the pan and cook, turning once, until the cheese melts. Keep quesadillas warm in the oven or in a pan on the indirect side of the grill.

4   Cut each quesadilla into wedges and serve warm with sour cream and salsa.

EXTRA POINTS Remember to carry a large nonstick skillet to the tailgate if you're preparing this on site.

Nutty Blue Cheese Ball

Whether shaped like a basketball, football, or even a racecar tire, cheese balls are a perennial favorite for event-day snacking. This one combines the *tang* of blue cheese with the *crunch* of walnuts. Be sure to prepare it ahead of time so that it has time to firm up. SERVES 6

One 8-ounce package cream cheese, at room temperature
³/₄ cup crumbled blue cheese, at room temperature

¹/₂ teaspoon Dijon mustard
2 tablespoons chopped fresh chives
¹/₂ cup chopped walnuts
Crackers of your choice for serving

1 Place the cream cheese, blue cheese, and mustard in a food processor. Process until smooth. Add the chives and pulse just to blend.

2 Place a sheet of plastic wrap on a clean work surface. Spread the chopped walnuts in the center of the sheet in a single layer. Mound the cheese mixture on top of the walnuts and pull the plastic wrap around it, pressing and rolling to adhere the nuts to the cheese.

3 Twist the plastic wrap to help shape the cheese into a ball, or your preferred shape, then seal with the plastic wrap. Refrigerate for several hours or overnight. Serve with crackers.

EXTRA POINTS You can prepare and refrigerate the cheese ball up to 3 days before your tailgate. Keep the cheese ball well chilled while transporting it and during serving.

Marylynn's Okra Roll-Ups

As I strolled through the tailgate scene at the Brookhill Steeplechase in Clayton, North Carolina, I spotted these *unusual* snacks, which use that Southern treat, pickled okra. Marylynn Rich of Youngsville, North Carolina, told me that these are a favorite of hers at tailgating events. Could you call them Southern sushi rolls? Sure 'nuff.   MAKES ABOUT 60 PIECES

One 16-ounce jar pickled okra, drained
10 ounces thinly sliced ham

One 8-ounce tub soft cream cheese

1   Pat the okra pods dry. Trim the stems and tips from the pods.

2   On a cutting board, spread 1 ham slice flat without tearing it. Gently spread a thin layer of cream cheese on the ham. Place 1 trimmed okra pod at one end of the slice and roll the ham up around it, pressing gently to make a tight roll. Trim any overhanging ham to fit the pod, then slice the roll into approximately ½-inch-long slices. Repeat with remaining okra pods. Keep chilled until ready to serve.

EXTRA POINTS Make these snacks the night before the tailgate, and refrigerate them in an airtight container. Store them in a single layer or multiple layers separated by waxed paper to prevent sticking.

Munchable Marinated Shrimp

These *spicy*, do-ahead goodies could be either the *centerpiece* of a party spread or a supporting player. Serve them on salad greens that you have tossed with vinaigrette—and a little feta cheese sprinkled on top wouldn't hurt, either. Toothpicks will make it easy to spear the shrimp.   SERVES 8 TO 10

3 quarts water

One 3-ounce box crab or shrimp boil-in-a-bag, such as Zatarain's

3 limes

2 pounds medium-size shrimp

$3/4$ cup olive oil

$1/4$ cup sherry vinegar

$3/4$ teaspoon whole celery seed

$3/4$ teaspoon red pepper flakes

$1/4$ teaspoon whole yellow mustard seed

$1/2$ cup chopped green onions

1 tablespoon drained capers

2 cloves garlic, crushed

Salt and freshly ground black pepper to taste

2 tablespoons chopped fresh flat-leaf parsley

1   Pour the water into a large saucepan. Add the crab boil-in-a-bag, squeeze in the juice of 1 lime, and toss in the squeezed halves. Bring to a boil. Add the shrimp and cook for 2 to 3 minutes, just until the shrimp are pink and done. Drain, discard the lime halves and crab boil, then plunge the shrimp into ice water to stop cooking. When the shrimp are cool enough to handle, drain, peel, and devein them, place in a large bowl, and set aside.

2   In a medium-size bowl, combine the juice of the remaining 2 limes, the olive oil, vinegar, celery seed, red pepper flakes, mustard seed, green onions, capers, and garlic. Add salt and pepper. Pour this mixture over the shrimp and stir to coat. Cover the bowl tightly with a lid or plastic wrap and refrigerate for 4 to 8 hours. Stir occasionally to keep all the shrimp coated with the seasoning.

3   When ready to serve, sprinkle the parsley over the top.

EXTRA POINTS Keep this dish well chilled, in the center of your cooler, on the way to the tailgate. Serve the shrimp in a bowl nestled in a larger bowl filled with ice to keep it cool.

Jo Ann's Campfire Onion Blossoms

These onions have all the *great* flavor of the famous beloved snack, without the need for the deep fryer. Race Mama Jo Ann Hlavac cooks these while camping before a NASCAR race. SERVES 4

4 large sweet onions, such as Vidalia,
OSO Sweet, or Texas 1050
1/4 cup (1/2 stick) unsalted butter

4 cloves garlic
Salt and freshly ground black pepper to taste
Ranch-style dip or hot pepper sauce (optional)

1   Light a hot fire in a charcoal grill.

2   Peel the onions and cut each one into quarters, but slice only about halfway down so that the onions will hold together. Place 1 tablespoon of butter and 1 clove of garlic in the middle of each onion.

3   Double-wrap each onion in aluminum foil and place directly on the hot coals of the grill. Cook for 30 to 40 minutes or until the onions are tender when pierced with a knife.

4   Carefully remove the foil-wrapped onions from the coals and unwrap. Season with salt and pepper. Onion wedges can be pulled apart and dipped into ranch-style dip or hot sauce, if desired.

EXTRA POINTS If you want to save some time, you can peel, quarter, and refrigerate the onions the day before the tailgate.

Slam-Dunk Sausage Balls

These are the sausage balls that started it all. *Express your opinion* by flinging one of these at the TV set, if you're willing to sacrifice a snack this easy and good. I keep a steady supply in the freezer throughout basketball season, ready to feed crowds large or small.   MAKES ABOUT 40 SAUSAGE BALLS

1 pound spicy pork bulk sausage
2 cups baking mix, such as Bisquick

1 cup shredded cheddar cheese

1   Preheat the oven to 400°F.

2   In a large bowl, using your hands, thoroughly combine the sausage, baking mix, and cheese. Roll the mixture into approximately 1-inch balls, and place the balls on rimmed baking sheets.

3   Bake for 10 to 12 minutes, or until the balls are lightly browned and cooked through. Serve hot or warm.

EXTRA POINTS If not serving immediately, you can cool the sausage balls completely, then place them in zipper-top plastic bags and freeze. To reheat, remove the number you need from the freezer and place directly in the microwave. Heat the sausage balls in 1-minute increments just until they are warmed through. Do not overheat or they may become tough. At an outdoor tailgate, wrap them in aluminum foil and place them on a corner of a grill to warm.

Thomas's Tennessee Cocktail

University of Georgia fan Thomas Lanford, Jr., starts working on his menus for the football-tailgating season in late spring or early summer. He serves this drink *before a game* against the Bulldogs' rival, the University of Tennessee.   SERVES 2

Cracked ice

4 ounces rye whiskey

2 ounces maraschino liqueur

2 ounces freshly squeezed lemon juice

Fill a cocktail shaker halfway full with cracked ice. Add the whiskey, maraschino liqueur, and lemon juice, and shake well. Strain into 2 chilled cocktail glasses.

Satan's Whiskers

This recipe, like the previous one, is from University of Georgia fan Thomas Lanford Jr., who says: "Satan's Whiskers is *in honor of* University of South Carolina football coach Steve Spurrier, who most University of Georgia fans believe is Satan incarnate." Ah, *the rivalry!* SERVES 2

Cracked ice

1 ounce gin

1 ounce dry vermouth

1 ounce sweet vermouth

1 ounce freshly squeezed orange juice

4 teaspoons orange curaçao or Grand Marnier

2 teaspoons orange bitters

2 orange twists, for garnish

Fill a cocktail shaker halfway full with cracked ice. Add the gin, dry vermouth, sweet vermouth, orange juice, curaçao, and bitters, and shake well. Strain into 2 chilled cocktail glasses and garnish each with an orange twist.

Brookhill Iced Tea

Mint juleps are traditional at the Kentucky Derby, but I wanted to come up with something a little different when I attended the Brookhill Steeplechase in Clayton, North Carolina. You will like the *hint of mint* and lemony flavor in this cooling beverage.   SERVES 8

2 quarts water

6 black tea bags

1½ cups Homemade Limoncello (recipe follows)

8 sprigs fresh mint, for garnish

8 lemon slices, for garnish

1   In a large saucepan, bring the water to a boil over high heat. Remove from the heat, add the tea bags, and let steep for 5 minutes. Discard the tea bags, let the tea cool, and refrigerate until completely chilled.

2   Fill 8 tall glasses with ice cubes. Pour about 1 cup of tea into each glass, then add 3 tablespoons limoncello to each glass; stir. Drop a mint sprig into each glass and garnish with a lemon slice.

EXTRA POINTS You can brew and refrigerate the tea 1 day before the tailgate. The Homemade Limoncello will keep in the freezer indefinitely.

HOMEMADE LIMONCELLO

There are dozens of recipes out there for this *digestivo* that originated in Italy. Some add one grated lime to the mix for bitterness, and others infuse the sugar syrup with lemon as well. This is a recipe I've used many times, with *great success*. The empty vodka bottles, washed and dried thoroughly, are good for storing the finished limoncello, though you will need more than the two bottles.   MAKES ABOUT 2 QUARTS

20 lemons
Two 750-milliliter bottles vodka

2 cups sugar
2 cups cold water

1   Grate the zest, avoiding the bitter white pith, from the lemons. Get the peel as fine as possible, using either a microplane grater or a regular grater and then chopping up the zest. Place the zest in a large, clean glass jar. Pour in 1 bottle of the vodka and shake. Place the jar in a cool, dark place for at least 2 weeks, shaking occasionally.

2   When the zest has lost its color and the vodka has turned yellow, the mixture is ready. It should smell fragrantly lemony. Strain the vodka through cheesecloth into another large, clean glass jar, pressing or squeezing the zest to remove all the oils. Stir in the second bottle of vodka.

3   Prepare a simple syrup by placing the sugar and water in a saucepan over low heat. Stir until the sugar has dissolved. Raise the heat to high and boil the syrup for 1 minute. Remove from the heat and let cool to room temperature.

4   Stir the cooled simple syrup into the lemon-infused vodka. Use a funnel to pour the limoncello into bottles for storage. Store in the freezer.

Lynchburg Lemonade

This recipe, from Fred Thompson's book *Lemonade: 50 Cool Recipes for Classic, Flavored, and Hard Lemonades and Sparklers* (The Harvard Common Press, 2002), jazzes up a *refreshing* Southern classic. Serve it any time you need to cool off during a heated game, race, or match. SERVES 2

Cracked ice as needed

4 ounces Jack Daniel's Black Label Sour-Mash whiskey or other similar whiskey

4 ounces Grand Marnier

4 ounces of your favorite lemonade

About 4 ounces carbonated citrus-flavored soda or club soda

2 sprigs fresh mint, for garnish (optional)

2 long-stemmed maraschino cherries, for garnish (optional)

1   Fill 2 tall 10-ounce glasses with cracked ice.

2   To each glass, add 2 ounces Jack Daniel's, 2 ounces Grand Marnier, and 2 ounces lemonade, and stir. Top each glass off with the citrus-flavored soda (for a less sweet version, use the club soda). Garnish each with a mint sprig and a cherry, if desired.

The Art of the Mint Julep

*B*efore the horses arrive, big, plastic cups full of sweet liquor are in the hands of fans at Churchill Downs. The mint julep—whose prime ingredient, bourbon, originated in Kentucky—is unbreakably linked with this classic sporting event, whether you're there in person or watching at home. But it's also one of the nation's most maligned drinks, because it's one of the most poorly prepared.

"The mint julep is to Southerners what the tea ceremony is to the Japanese. It's a performance and presentation that transcends the beverage, its assembly, or even its consumption," says Elliott Warnock of Chapel Hill, North Carolina. Elliott is a card-carrying Kentucky Colonel, a title bestowed by Kentucky's governor. Members of the Honorable Order of Kentucky Colonels from across the country and around the world have been doing charitable works, and organizing parties at the Derby, since before World War II.

It's a lot of work to make mint juleps properly. Also, it's hard to make just one. Mint juleps are a social occasion. And, yes, it is a sweet drink. But if you make it right, with enough bourbon, you won't care.

Elliott says there are two schools of julep making, depending on personal preference. For the first version, prepare a simple syrup: two cups sugar in two cups of water, heated on low and stirred to dissolve the sugar, then boiled for one minute. Then, toss in a few sprigs of fresh mint and refrigerate overnight. Remove the sprigs before using the syrup. To prepare the drinks, you'll need silver or pewter tumblers called Jefferson cups or julep cups. Gently crush two or three leaves of fresh mint in each cup, but don't shred the leaves. Pack the cups with very finely crushed or shaved ice. Immediately add two to two-and-a-half ounces of bourbon. Kentucky bourbon, of course. Then fill with the mint-flavored syrup, stir lightly, and top with a fresh sprig of mint (use a cocktail straw or small spoon to poke a hole in the ice, if necessary). Sip, and enjoy the cool feeling as the cup frosts over.

For the second version, use tall, opaque glasses instead of cups. Gently crush a few leaves of mint in the bottom of each glass, mashing a little harder than in the first version, and cover with one-half to three-quarters of an inch of confectioners' sugar, along with just enough water to stir and dissolve the sugar. Pack the glass with the crushed or shaved ice, pour in bourbon to the rim, and garnish with a sprig of mint. Allow the ice to melt a little, then sip with caution.

Elliott offers this final warning: "A real mint julep is not to be toyed with or tinkered about. Do not add pineapple, or lemon zest, or orange slices. To do so is to risk banishment from the South." Got that, y'all?

Blue Lagoon

This *tropical* cooler is from Fred Thompson's book *Lemonade: 50 Cool Recipes for Classic, Flavored, and Hard Lemonades and Sparklers* (The Harvard Common Press, 2002). I might call it a Carolina Blue Lagoon, if serving it during a Tar Heels game. For variety, Fred suggests substituting lemon-flavored vodka or rum for the plain vodka. Use from-scratch or from-concentrate lemonade, not a mix, for this beverage.

SERVES 2

Ice cubes
3 ounces vodka

2 ounces blue curaçao
²/₃ cup lemonade

Add several ice cubes to a cocktail shaker or any jar with a lid (a Mason jar works great). Add the vodka, blue curaçao, and lemonade, and shake until cold. Strain into 2 oversize martini glasses or serve on the rocks in highball glasses.

EXTRA POINTS You can make the lemonade 1 day before the tailgate and mix the drink up just before serving.

Denise's Mimosas

As I adjusted my flowered hat and prepared to view the Brookhill Steeplechase in Clayton, North Carolina, my friend Denise Rhodes served these mimosas at a prerace brunch. Mimosas are *traditional* libations at elegant sports-related brunches, and these are as gorgeously colored as springtime flowers. SERVES 1

1 maraschino cherry

1 tablespoon grenadine syrup

1 part chilled freshly squeezed orange juice

1 part chilled brut champagne

Drop the maraschino cherry into the bottom of a champagne flute. Add the grenadine, then fill the flute halfway with the orange juice. Add champagne to the top of the flute. Do not stir or the champagne will lose its bubbles. These are best made fresh, one at a time.

Eddie's Bloody Mary

My old friend Eddie Yandle gave me a classic recipe for
Bloody Marys many years ago. Over the course of many
Atlantic Coast Conference Basketball Tournament brunches,
I have modified it into this *winning* version. SERVES 10 TO 12

7 to 8 pounds ripe tomatoes or 2 quarts organic,
  no-salt-added pure tomato juice
2 teaspoons Worcestershire sauce
3 to 4 dashes hot pepper sauce, to your taste
1 teaspoon prepared horseradish

2 teaspoons freshly squeezed lemon juice
1 beef bouillon cube, crushed (low salt,
  if available)
5 to 7 ounces vodka, to your taste
10 to 12 celery sticks, for garnish

1   If using fresh tomatoes, cut them into quarters and puree in a blender in batches.
Strain to remove the seeds, pulp, and skin. You should end up with 2 quarts of juice.

2   Combine the tomato juice, Worcestershire sauce, hot pepper sauce, horseradish,
lemon juice, bouillon, and vodka in a large pitcher and stir well to combine. Serve over ice
cubes in tall glasses, garnishing each drink with a celery stick.

EXTRA POINTS The mix can be prepared and refrigerated in a glass screw-top
jar the night before the tailgate. Shake to combine before serving. The fresh
tomato juice can also be made the day before serving. If you prefer, you can leave
the vodka out of the pitcher when mixing the Bloody Mary ingredients and allow
guests to add their own according to their taste.

Whassup, Mary?

A Bloody Mary is the drink of choice at sports-watching brunches. This one brings a fresh flavor and Asian fire to the old girl. It does take some time to make fresh tomato juice, but the difference is *amazing*—and it can be made 24 hours ahead. Look for bottled ginger juice and wasabi powder in the Asian food section of a large supermarket and in specialty markets. A long green onion makes a great swizzle stick. SERVES 6 TO 8

3½ to 4 pounds ripe tomatoes
3½ teaspoons wasabi powder
1 tablespoon plus 1 teaspoon ginger juice
1½ teaspoons salt

2 tablespoons freshly squeezed lemon juice
3 to 4 ounces vodka, to your taste
6 to 8 long green onions, roots trimmed, for garnish

1   Cut the tomatoes into quarters and puree in a blender in batches. Strain to remove the seeds, pulp, and skin. You should end up with 1 quart of juice.

2   Combine the tomato juice, wasabi powder, ginger juice, salt, and lemon juice in a large pitcher and stir well to combine. Add the vodka and stir.

3   To serve, pour the mixture over ice cubes into tall glasses. Add 1 green onion to each glass for garnish.

EXTRA POINTS The mix can be prepared and refrigerated in a glass screw-top jar the night before the tailgate. Shake to combine before serving.

Smokin' Mary

If you don't have time to make tomato juice, don't fall back on muddy-flavored, salty mixers or thick canned juices. Look for a bottled *all-natural*, no-salt-added pure tomato juice at organic or specialty markets. I prefer not to add vodka to the juice mixture, which allows guests to tailor drinks to their own tastes and lets those who want a Virgin Mary join in the fun. SERVES 6 TO 8

3¹/₂ to 4 pounds ripe tomatoes or 1 quart organic, no-salt-added pure tomato juice
1 tablespoon plus 1 teaspoon chipotle puree (see Extra Points)
¹/₃ cup freshly squeezed lime juice
1¹/₂ teaspoons salt
1 teaspoon garlic powder
Vodka to taste
6 to 8 sprigs fresh cilantro, for garnish
6 to 8 lime slices, for garnish

1   If using fresh tomatoes, cut them into quarters and puree in a blender in batches. Strain to remove the seeds, pulp, and skin. You should end up with 1 quart of juice.

2   Combine the tomato juice, chipotle puree, lime juice, salt, and garlic powder in a large pitcher and stir well to combine.

3   To serve, pour the mixture over ice cubes into tall glasses and stir in the desired amount of vodka. Crush in a sprig of cilantro, stir, and garnish the rim of each glass with a slice of lime.

EXTRA POINTS To make chipotle puree, place a can of chipotle chiles in adobo sauce in a blender and process until smooth. Seal leftovers in a plastic bag and refrigerate or freeze.

Red-Hot Cider

I think that almost everything can be improved by the judicious addition of hot peppers, and that is true of this cider. This is a real pre- or postgame *warm-up*, and the recipe can easily be doubled for a large crowd (or if it's really cold out). The cranberry juice moderates the sweetness of the apple cider.   SERVES 8

2 cinnamon sticks, broken in half
8 whole cloves
10 whole allspice berries
Half of a dried chile de arbol or Thai chile,
   stem and seeds removed

1 large strip orange peel, approximately
   4 x 2 inches
1 quart apple cider
$1/2$ cup cranberry juice

1   Place the cinnamon sticks, cloves, allspice berries, chile, and orange peel on a small square of cheesecloth. Tie the cheesecloth closed with a piece of kitchen twine.

2   In a large saucepan, stir together the apple cider and cranberry juice. Bring to a boil, then reduce the heat to a low simmer, add the spice bag, and cover. Simmer for 30 minutes, or until the spice flavor is as strong as you like. Remove and discard the bag of spices. Serve hot.

EXTRA POINTS Take this to the tailgate in a large thermos. If watching the big game at home, keep the beverage warm in a slow cooker set on LOW, but remove the spice bag so the cider will not be too spicy.

Soups, Beans, and Chili

No plates are needed for these recipes.
Every *fabulous* Super Bowl party calls

for some wonderful chili or soup—served individually

in deep bowls or hearty mugs—to keep the fans

warmed up for action. Or, bring out the family-style

big bowls for a *lavish seafood boil*.

Whether your crowd includes famished carnivores or

veggie fans, there are recipes here for them, with

flavors from *hot* and *spicy* to *mild* and *mellow*. Also, most are easy to prepare ahead of time, so the cook won't miss a minute of the action.

Number One Sweet Potato Soup	46	Quick Bean Medley for a Crowd	55	
Don't Tell Them It's Good for Them Vegetable Soup	47	Party Time Red Beans and Rice	56	
Black Bean and Corn Soup	48	Big Feed Jambalaya	58	
Foy's Patriot Clam Chowder	50	Very Veggie Lentil Chili	60	
Carolina Champions Shrimp Bowl	52	Lucy's Stout Steak Chili	62	
John's Corn Chowder	53	Marvelous Mole Chili	64	
New Year's Day Baked Beans	54	Smokin' Chicken Chili	66	

Number One Sweet Potato Soup

I gave my neighbor, Kathy Hedberg, this recipe, and she said her teenage son, John, liked it so much that he requested the soup as his *birthday meal*. She told me that you've really accomplished something when a teenager likes what you've cooked, so I feel this is definitely a number-one soup. It is also an unexpectedly crowd-pleasing addition to any winter sports party.   SERVES 6

2 pounds sweet potatoes
3 tablespoons unsalted butter
1 cup chopped onions
3 cups chicken broth
$^1/_2$ teaspoon grated fresh ginger
1 teaspoon curry powder

$^1/_2$ teaspoon ground cinnamon
1 clove garlic, chopped
Salt and freshly ground black pepper to taste
Cream or half-and-half (optional)
Chopped toasted pecans (optional)

1   Peel and slice the sweet potatoes. Place in a large saucepan or stockpot, cover with water, and bring to a boil. Reduce the heat to a simmer and cook until tender when pierced with a fork. Drain and set aside.

2   Wipe out the pot, return to medium-low heat, and add the butter to melt it. Add the chopped onions and cook slowly, stirring often, to caramelize the onions, about 10 minutes.

3   Return the potatoes to the pot and add the chicken broth, using enough to cover the potatoes (you may need slightly less or more than 3 cups). Add the ginger, curry powder, cinnamon, and garlic. Take the pot off the heat and puree the mixture with a stick blender, or carefully pour it into a regular blender and puree. Add salt and pepper. Return to the heat and bring to a boil over high heat, stirring. Add more chicken broth or water if the mixture is too thick for your liking.

4   Reduce the heat and simmer for a few minutes to let the flavors blend, or let the soup sit over low heat, covered, until you're ready to serve. Serve as is or, if desired, swirl a teaspoon of cream into each bowl and top with chopped pecans.

EXTRA POINTS Stock the freezer with this soup and reheat it in a pot on the grill or gas burner to warm up a cold game day.

Don't Tell Them It's Good for Them Vegetable Soup

Sometimes you have to *sneak* a little *nutrition* onto the fan training table. After all, fans need to eat well to keep up their strength for the playoffs or those green-white checkered finishes. SERVES 6 TO 8

1/4 cup olive oil

2 cups chopped onion

2 cups chopped celery

2 cups chopped carrots

1 clove garlic, chopped

1 quart chicken broth

One 14.5-ounce can diced tomatoes, undrained

1 cup peeled, diced potatoes

Salt and freshly ground black pepper to taste

1 cup shredded green cabbage

1　Heat the olive oil in a large stockpot or Dutch oven over medium heat. Add the onions, celery, carrots, and garlic. Cook, stirring, until the vegetables are soft but not browned, about 5 minutes.

2　Add the chicken broth, tomatoes with their juice, and potatoes, plus enough water to cover the vegetables by about 2 inches. Add salt and pepper. Bring the mixture to a boil, then reduce the heat, cover, and simmer for 30 minutes.

3　Add the cabbage, stir, and simmer for another 5 to 10 minutes, or until the cabbage is soft. Serve hot.

EXTRA POINTS You can prep and refrigerate the onion, celery, carrots, potatoes, and cabbage the day before the tailgate, storing them in zipper-top plastic bags, then easily prepare the soup on site over a gas grill or gas burner. Or you can make the soup ahead and refrigerate for up to 2 days or freeze for up to 6 months.

Black Bean and Corn Soup

Sports fans, this soup is as *hearty* as any meat-filled chili and carries a *punch* of flavor. You might actually feel healthy eating it. Multiply the proportions if you need to feed a crowd, and substitute water for the chicken broth if feeding strict vegetarians. Note that you need to presoak the dried beans for this recipe.   SERVES 6 TO 8

1 pound dried black beans, rinsed and
   picked over
1 quart chicken broth
1 medium-size onion, chopped
2 garlic cloves, chopped
One 16-ounce can chopped tomatoes, undrained
2 canned chipotle chiles in adobo sauce,
   plus 1 teaspoon adobo sauce from can

¹/₂ cup chopped fresh cilantro
1 cup corn (fresh, frozen, or drained canned)
Juice from ¹/₂ lime
Salt to taste
Sour cream for garnish
Shredded Monterey Jack cheese for garnish

1   Place the beans in a bowl, add water to cover by at least 1 inch, and soak for 6 hours or overnight.

2   Drain the beans and put them in a large soup pot. Add the chicken broth and enough cold water to cover the beans by a couple of inches. Bring to a boil, skimming off the foam that rises to the surface. Add the onion and garlic. Lower the heat and simmer until the onions are soft, about 15 minutes.

3   While the beans are simmering, place the tomatoes with their juice, chipotles, and adobo sauce in a food processor. Pulse until blended but still chunky.

4   At the end of the 15 minutes, add the tomato mixture, ¹/₄ cup of the cilantro, the corn, and the lime juice to the pot. Simmer, stirring occasionally, until the beans are tender, about 1 hour. When done, add salt and stir in the remaining ¹/₄ cup cilantro. Serve the sour cream and the cheese on the side.

EXTRA POINTS Prepare this soup the day before the tailgate and simply reheat it at game time.

All Aboard the Cockabooses

*E*lite fans at the University of South Carolina in Columbia don't tailgate, they "railgate." That's what game day aboard one of the 22 Cockabooses has come to be called.

The Cockabooses are actual cabooses, parked on a defunct rail line that's a Hail Mary pass away from the entrance to Williams-Brice Stadium. Outside, each 30 x 9-foot car is painted an identical Gamecock garnet with gold team logos. Inside, they're as elaborate as money and fan devotion can make them. Mahogany cabinetry, brass appointments, built-in stereo systems, Victorian upholstery, and fancy countertops abound. Each is wired and has plumbing, heating, and air conditioning. It's not unheard of for an owner to spend $100,000 or more to trick out his Cockaboose.

In the 1990s, a local businessman purchased the shabby, unused tracks near the stadium and started acquiring the cabooses. The original owners purchased the cars for around $40,000 each. Today, the price for a Cockaboose can range easily into the mid-six figures, if one should come up for sale.

As for food, most owners leave that to the pros. Many hire chefs and bartenders to provide refreshment before and after they enjoy a home game or, if the Gamecocks are playing out of town, while watching on their big-screen TVs.

Foy's Patriot Clam Chowder

Fellow cook Foy Allen Edelman of Raleigh, North Carolina, came up with this recipe for a Super Bowl cookoff held when the New England Patriots won in 2001. Participants were asked to prepare dishes representing the teams playing, which is a fun and different theme for a Super Bowl party. Foy says of the chowder, "It has a *hearty aroma* that sends my taste buds straight to the sea!" SERVES 4 TO 6

½ cup (1 stick) unsalted butter (or 4 slices bacon or 2 to 3 ounces salt pork)

2 to 2½ cups peeled white potatoes cut into ½-inch cubes

½ cup chopped onions

1 large stalk celery, chopped

½ cup all-purpose flour

8 ounces all-natural clam juice

Two 6.5-ounce cans minced or chopped clams, undrained

1 cup heavy cream

Salt and freshly ground black pepper to taste

Chopped fresh flat-leaf parsley for garnish

1   In a 3-quart stockpot or Dutch oven over medium heat, melt the butter. If using bacon or salt pork, fry it over medium heat until crispy, then remove, let cool, chop, and set aside, leaving the drippings in the pot.

2   Add the potatoes, onions, and celery to the pot. Sauté the mixture for 10 to 15 minutes over medium heat, stirring to prevent sticking.

3   When the onions are soft and the potatoes begin to brown, sprinkle the flour over the vegetables and stir it in for 1 to 2 minutes, or until the mixture gets very thick. Keep turning and stirring the mixture to completely blend in the flour.

4   Pour in the clam juice, stirring continuously. As soon as the mixture is well blended and smooth, add the clams with their juice. Fill one of the empty clam cans with water and add the water to the pot. Stir until the mixture is smooth and hot. Pour in the cream,

stirring continuously. As soon as the mixture is well blended, turn the heat to very low. Do not let the cream overheat, or it will curdle. When the chowder is hot, season with salt and pepper.

5   Garnish individual servings with parsley and the reserved chopped bacon or salt pork, if using. Serve hot.

EXTRA POINTS **You can prep the potatoes, onions, and celery the night before the tailgate and refrigerate them in zipper-top plastic bags. Then you can easily prepare the chowder on site over a gas burner.**

Carolina Champions Shrimp Bowl

This is my version of a *classic* coastal combination called Frogmore Stew, a South Carolina seafood dish. Some recipes include smoked sausage, but I prefer the lighter flavor without it. The great thing about this meal is that you just put the big serving bowl on the table, toss out some napkins, and let everyone dig in. You don't need much else, except maybe a salad on the side. SERVES 6

3 lemons, each cut in half
1 package crab boil-in-a-bag, such as Zatarain's
2 pounds small red or new potatoes, unpeeled
1 medium-size yellow onion
3 large cloves garlic, crushed
3 tablespoons Old Bay seasoning

2 teaspoons hot pepper sauce
3 large or 4 small ears fresh corn, shucked and cleaned
1½ pounds medium-size shrimp
Melted butter, seafood cocktail sauce, and lemon wedges for serving (optional)

1   Add the lemon halves and crab boil-in-a-bag to a large pot of water and bring to a boil. The pot needs to be big enough to hold all the ingredients, which you will add in stages; don't overfill with water.

2   Cut the potatoes into quarters, making sure the pieces are roughly the same size. Cut the onion into quarters.

3   When the water comes to a boil, add the potatoes, onion, garlic, Old Bay, and hot pepper sauce. Cover, reduce the heat to medium, and simmer for about 10 minutes, or until a knife easily pierces the potatoes.

4   Break the ears of corn into pieces about 3 inches long. Add the corn to the pot, return to a boil, and cook, uncovered, for about 1 minute. Add the shrimp and stir. Cook for 1 to 2 minutes, or until the shrimp turn pink and are cooked through; be careful not to overcook.

5   Drain immediately in a large strainer. Discard the crab boil bag and lemon halves, and pour everything into a large serving bowl. Serve hot or warm, with melted butter, seafood cocktail sauce, and lemon wedges, if desired.

EXTRA POINTS Gather the tailgate gang around and make cooking this dish a party. The large pot of a turkey fryer is great for making this treat.

John's Corn Chowder

John White, husband of my friend Elizabeth Swaringen, of Pittsboro, North Carolina, prepares this soup to *cure whatever ails you*—maybe even your team's tragic loss to an archrival.   SERVES 6

1 cup whole milk

6 tablespoons all-purpose flour

One 10-ounce can premium chunk white chicken, undrained

One 15-ounce can cream-style yellow corn

One 15.25-ounce can yellow whole-kernel corn, undrained

2 cups frozen hash browns

Two 14.5-ounce cans reduced-sodium chicken broth

$1/2$ cup chopped yellow onions

1 cup chopped red bell peppers

Salt and freshly ground black pepper to taste

1   Place the milk and flour in a 4-quart saucepan and whisk together. Add the chicken, cream-style corn, whole-kernel corn, hash browns, chicken broth, onions, and red peppers and stir until well combined.

2   Place the saucepan over medium heat and bring to a simmer. Simmer for 15 minutes, or until hot and thick, stirring occasionally. Add salt and pepper. Serve hot.

EXTRA POINTS Chop the onions and red peppers the night before the tailgate and refrigerate in zipper-top plastic bags. Then prepare this easy soup at the tailgate. Don't forget the can opener for this one!

New Year's Day Baked Beans

This is a *great side dish* for New Year's Day bowl-game watching. The beans can sit in the slow cooker, keeping warm throughout the afternoon. If there's no time to presoak the beans, you can soften them by boiling and simmering them instead (see step 1). The key is to soften the dried beans before cooking them with the other ingredients. SERVES 10

1¹/₂ pounds dried navy beans, rinsed and
  picked over
1 medium-size yellow onion, chopped
1¹/₂ cups ketchup
1¹/₂ cups light brown sugar

1¹/₂ cups water
1 tablespoon ground mustard
¹/₄ cup molasses
Salt to taste

1   Soak the beans for 8 hours in water to cover by about 2 inches. (Or place them in a saucepan with water to cover, boil for 10 minutes, then reduce the heat, cover, and simmer for 1¹/₂ hours, until the beans are tender.) Drain.

2   Place the beans in a 4¹/₂-quart slow cooker. In a small bowl, combine the onion, ketchup, brown sugar, water, ground mustard, and molasses. Add to the beans and stir well. Cover and cook on the LOW setting for 10 to 12 hours (it will probably take closer to 12 hours). Stir occasionally near the end of the cooking time. Before serving, add salt.

EXTRA POINTS These beans can be cooked a day ahead of time and reheated in a saucepan on low heat, either at home on the stove or on the corner of the grill at the tailgate.

Quick Bean Medley for a Crowd

This dish is a great twist on traditional baked beans, and it is an *easy way to fuel* the tailgate crew. The recipe comes from *Desperation Entertaining!* (Workman Publishing, 2002), written by my good friends Alicia Ross and Beverly Mills. SERVES 12

One 15-ounce can pinto beans, undrained
One 15-ounce can red kidney beans, undrained
One 15-ounce can navy beans, undrained
One 15-ounce can chickpeas, drained
1 large onion, chopped

1 green bell pepper, chopped
3 tablespoons honey
2 tablespoons Dijon mustard
2 teaspoons olive oil
2 teaspoons minced garlic

1   Preheat the oven to 350°F.

2   Spray a 9 x 13-inch baking dish or a 3-quart casserole dish with nonstick cooking spray. Add the pinto beans, kidney beans, and navy beans, with their liquids, the drained chickpeas, onion, green pepper, honey, mustard, oil, and garlic to the dish. Stir gently but thoroughly, until the ingredients are mixed.

3   Bake, uncovered, until beans are bubbly and the onions and green pepper are tender, 30 to 35 minutes. Serve hot.

EXTRA POINTS Reheat this in a heavy pot on a gas grill at the tailgate. Leftovers store well, covered, in the refrigerator for several days, and the dish's flavor actually improves. Or you can assemble and refrigerate the dish the day before the tailgate, then bake it shortly before serving.

Party Time Red Beans and Rice

Red beans and rice is a Louisiana classic that feeds a party and keeps fans *cheering*. I offer this dish along with Big Feed Jambalaya (page 58) at my annual Christmas party. And make some extra Salt-Free Cajun Seasoning—it's great on everything from grilled chicken to fried fish to deviled eggs, and it's a good rub for Fast Lane Fried Turkey (page 82). Use a Louisiana brand of red beans, if you can find one. I adapted this recipe from one in *Louisiana Real and Rustic* (William Morrow, 1996) by Emeril Lagasse. SERVES 8

1 pound dried red kidney beans, rinsed and
   picked over
2 tablespoons vegetable oil
1 cup chopped onions
1/2 cup chopped green bell peppers
1/2 cup chopped celery
1 teaspoon salt

4 bay leaves
2 tablespoons Salt-Free Cajun Seasoning
   (recipe follows)
3 tablespoons chopped garlic
1/2 teaspoon vinegar-based hot pepper sauce,
   or to taste (optional)
6 cups cooked rice

1 Place the beans in a large bowl and add enough water to cover by at least 1 inch. Let soak 8 hours or overnight.

2 Drain the beans. In a large saucepan or Dutch oven, heat the vegetable oil over medium-high heat. Add the onions, green peppers, celery, salt, bay leaves, and Salt-Free Cajun Seasoning and sauté for 5 to 6 minutes. Add the beans, garlic, and enough water to cover the contents in the pot by a couple of inches. Add hot pepper sauce, if desired.

3 Bring to a boil. Reduce the heat to medium and simmer, uncovered, stirring occasionally, for about 2 hours. Add water if the mixture becomes dry and thick.

4   After 2 hours, use a wooden spoon to mash about half of the mixture against the side of the pot, and stir to blend. Continue to cook uncovered, stirring occasionally, for another 1¹/₂ hours, or until the mixture is creamy and the beans are soft. Add more water if it becomes too thick. The mixture should be soupy, but not watery.

5   Remove the bay leaves and serve over cooked rice.

EXTRA POINTS **This dish can be cooked a day ahead, refrigerated, and reheated gently on a burner or grill over low heat. Wait until the last minute to combine the beans and rice, though.**

SALT-FREE CAJUN SEASONING

Make sure you use garlic and onion *powder*, not *salt*. Add more cayenne if you like it *hot*.   MAKES ABOUT ¹/₃ CUP

1 tablespoon plus 1¹/₂ teaspoons paprika
1 heaping tablespoon garlic powder
1¹/₂ teaspoons onion powder
1¹/₂ teaspoons cayenne pepper

1¹/₂ teaspoons dried marjoram or oregano
1¹/₂ teaspoons dried thyme
¹/₂ teaspoon hot chili powder

Combine all of the ingredients in a small bowl. Store in an airtight jar for up to 6 months. The spice mix may clump, but simply shake the jar to loosen it up.

Big Feed Jambalaya

Fans of the Louisiana State University Tigers in Baton Rouge *laissent les bon temps rouler* at tailgate time by simmering big pots of *gumbo* and jambalaya, classic *Cajun* dishes. Jambalaya is a great way to feed a crowd anytime—for more than 12 years, my husband and I have made it for upward of 30 people at our annual Christmas party. This is our version of a classic recipe that we learned from Joe Cahn, who now travels the country as the "Commissioner of Tailgating." Do not lift the lid while the rice is cooking or it will dry out.

SERVES 12

1/4 cup vegetable oil

2 1/2 to 3 pounds boneless chicken breast, cooked and shredded

1 1/2 pounds andouille sausage, diced

4 cups chopped onions

2 cups chopped celery

2 cups chopped green bell peppers

1 tablespoon chopped garlic

5 cups chicken broth

2 heaping teaspoons salt

1/2 heaping teaspoon cayenne pepper, or to taste

1/2 teaspoon vinegar-based hot pepper sauce, such as Tabasco, Crystal, or Vampfire, or more to taste

4 cups long-grain white rice (don't use converted rice)

1 Heat the vegetable oil in a large, heavy pot over medium-high heat. Add the chicken and heat, stirring, until lightly browned, 2 to 3 minutes. Add the sausage and cook, stirring, until lightly browned, about 5 minutes. Remove the sausage and chicken from the pot and set aside.

2 Add the onions, celery, green peppers, and garlic to the pot. Cook, stirring, until tender but not limp or browned, 5 to 6 minutes. Add a little more oil if needed to prevent sticking.

3 Return the chicken and sausage to the pot. Add the chicken broth, salt, cayenne pepper, and hot pepper sauce and bring to a boil. Add the rice, stir, and return to a boil.

4 When the mixture is boiling, cover, reduce the heat to low, and simmer for 10 minutes. Do not lift the lid during this time. At the end of 10 minutes, remove the lid and, using 2 large spoons, quickly turn the rice from top to bottom. Cover, turn off heat, and let sit for 20 more minutes. Do not lift the lid. At the end of 20 minutes, check to be sure all the liquid has been absorbed; if not, cover and let sit a few more minutes.

EXTRA POINTS Look for cooked chicken breast at your supermarket deli or prepared-foods counter. You can shred the chicken and chop the sausage and vegetables the night before, but the jambalaya is best made and served the same day. Some prefer brown or red jambalaya. For brown, add 1 tablespoon Kitchen Bouquet to the mixture at step 3. For red, replace half the chicken broth with tomato or tomato-vegetable juice and add about $1/4$ cup paprika at step 3.

Very Veggie Lentil Chili

Even meat-eating fans will be satisfied with this *thick*, rich chili. The flavors are *bold* enough to transform this lowly legume into a tailgate feast. I thank my friends Alicia Ross and Beverly Mills for this recipe from their cookbook *Cheap, Fast, Good!* (Workman Publishing, 2005). SERVES 6 TO 8

4 cups vegetable broth
1¹/₂ cups water
1 pound (about 2¹/₃ cups) brown lentils
One 14.5-ounce can diced tomatoes, undrained
1 cup chopped onions
4 cloves garlic, chopped
One 6-ounce can tomato paste
2 tablespoons ketchup
1 tablespoon chili powder
1¹/₂ teaspoons ground cumin

¹/₂ teaspoon dried thyme
¹/₂ teaspoon salt, or to taste
¹/₂ teaspoon freshly ground black pepper, or to taste
2 tablespoons olive oil
1 tablespoon balsamic vinegar
Hot pepper sauce to taste (optional)
Shredded cheddar cheese for serving
Sour cream for serving

1 Bring the broth and water to a boil in a 4¹/₂-quart Dutch oven or soup pot. When the broth comes to a boil, add the lentils, and bring the mixture back to a boil. Reduce the heat to low, cover, and simmer for 20 minutes. Partially uncover the pot if the mixture threatens to boil over.

2 Add the tomatoes with their juice, onions, garlic, tomato paste, ketchup, chili powder, cumin, thyme, salt, and black pepper. Stir to mix well. Simmer, covered, stirring frequently, for 15 minutes. Add a little more water or vegetable broth if all of the moisture evaporates.

3 Remove the pan from the heat and stir in the olive oil and vinegar. Add hot pepper sauce, if desired. Serve hot, topped with cheese and sour cream.

EXTRA POINTS Make the chili a day ahead and store, covered, in the refrigerator. Reheat in a heavy pot on a corner of the grill.

Step up to the Plate

The great American pastimes of tailgating and Major League Baseball rarely meet. Perhaps it's because many baseball stadiums are located in older, denser parts of cities, where parking is difficult and usually on the street rather than in spacious lots. Some stadiums with lots, like Yankee Stadium in New York, permit tailgating but ban grills and alcohol. (Then what's the point?)

At Miller Park, however, fans enjoy a baseball tailgating experience that rivals that of their Cheesehead brothers and sisters during football season. The only catch is: They're not necessarily Brewers fans.

Locals say that the ballpark becomes "Wrigley Field North" during the Brewers' home series with the Chicago Cubs. Tailgating is not allowed in the few Wrigley parking lots, so Miller Park's reputation for great tailgating draws Cubs fans in droves. Gloria Strehlow of Milwaukee has organized tailgates for as many as 50 folks—most of them Chicago fans. Actually, Gloria works both sides of the dugout. She's a Brewers fan for the season, except when the Cubs come to town. "Cubs fans can't believe it the first time they come out," she says. "Fans come in with loudspeakers playing the Cubs' fight song."

The Brewers' tailgating tradition goes back to their former home, Milwaukee County Stadium. Built in 1953, the older stadium seated about 36,000, plus patients at the nearby Veterans Administration hospital, who could watch games from their balconies. Tailgating for baseball games may have been sparked by the Green Bay Packers playing several games a season at the stadium until 1994. But whatever started it, tailgating became so popular that fans specifically requested that the new stadium allow for it. So, when the 43,000-seat Miller Park opened in 2001, it included plenty of room to spread out, plus permanent tailgating pavilions for private parties.

Today, there's an air of tolerance in the parking lot. Chicago and Milwaukee fans come together over grilling bratwurst, watching the kids play catch, and playing games of cornhole (a twist on horseshoes in which you toss a bag stuffed with dried corn at a hole in a wooden platform). If there can be peace at a tailgate on a summer afternoon, perhaps peace on Earth is not too much to hope for.

Lucy's Stout Steak Chili

You gotta have some great chili recipes for Super Bowl parties. This recipe is from Lucy Saunders, editor of www.beercook.com, a Web site devoted to craft beer and food. There are many more wonderful recipes in her upcoming cookbook, *Grilling with Beer*, which offers dozens of ways to use beer as an ingredient. Stout is a *strong, dark ale* made with roasted barley, which gives it a deep color and rich flavor. This chili cooks almost entirely in a slow cooker, so it's easy to make for a crowd. Use fresh or pickled jalapeños.   SERVES 8

1 tablespoon olive oil
3 pounds sirloin steak, trimmed of fat and cut
   into 1-inch cubes
1 cup chopped yellow onions
2 tablespoons minced garlic
One 15-ounce can black beans, undrained
One 15-ounce can pinto beans, undrained
One 15-ounce can red kidney beans, undrained
One 15-ounce can diced tomatoes, undrained
One 6-ounce can tomato paste
1½ cups chopped green bell peppers
1½ cups chopped red bell peppers
2 tablespoons minced jalapeños or other green
   chiles

1 cube low-sodium beef bouillon
12 ounces stout beer
3 tablespoons chili powder
1 teaspoon cayenne pepper
1 teaspoon ground cumin
1 teaspoon dried oregano
1 tablespoon molasses

GARNISHES (OPTIONAL)
Shredded cheddar cheese
Minced onions
Sliced black olives
Minced red bell peppers

1   Heat the oil in a large nonstick skillet over medium heat. Add the steak, onions, and garlic and sauté for 5 minutes, stirring often, until the meat is lightly browned and the onions are just tender. Do not overcook.

2   Scrape the contents of the skillet into a 4½-quart slow cooker. Add the black beans, pinto beans, and kidney beans with their liquids, the diced tomatoes with their juice, the tomato paste, green and red peppers, jalapeños, bouillon cube, stout, chili powder, cayenne

pepper, cumin, oregano, and molasses. Cover and cook on LOW for 4 to 6 hours, stirring occasionally.

3 Serve with the garnishes suggested above or those of your choice.

EXTRA POINTS If you like, you can make this rich chili a day ahead, refrigerate it, and reheat it at tailgate time. Reheat it on a burner or grill, though, rather than in the slow cooker, which doesn't get hot enough to reheat food properly. To find a good stout, check out the Brewers Association Web site, www.beertown.org, which offers a directory of craft brewers to help you locate a fresh stout brewed near you.

Marvelous Mole Chili

The mole sauces of Mexico and the dedicated all-beef (no beans) philosophy found at competitive chili cookoffs inspired this recipe. At a New Year's Day chili tasting, one of my guests dropped some *cornbread* into her bowl and loved the combination—try it! SERVES 6

5 dried ancho chiles

4 dried pasilla chiles

5 dried guajillo or New Mexico chiles

3 tablespoons vegetable oil

3 pounds beef chuck roast, cut into 1-inch cubes

1 cup chopped onions

1 tablespoon chopped garlic

One 8-ounce can tomato sauce

2 quarts chicken broth

1 bay leaf

$1/2$ teaspoon ground cinnamon

1 teaspoon dried oregano

$1/2$ teaspoon ground cumin

$1/4$ teaspoon cayenne pepper

Salt to taste

Cornbread for serving (optional)

1 Place the ancho, pasilla, and guajillo chiles in a bowl, cover with boiling water, and let soak for 30 minutes. Use a saucer to weigh them down if they float to the surface.

2 Meanwhile, heat 1 tablespoon of the vegetable oil in a large saucepan or Dutch oven over medium heat. Lightly brown the beef; do not overcook. Remove the beef from the pan, draining any liquid, and set aside.

3 Heat the remaining 2 tablespoons oil in the same pan and cook the onions and garlic until soft, but not browned. Remove the pan from the heat.

4 When the chiles have soaked for 30 minutes, drain them, remove the stems and seeds (hold under running water to do this), and pat dry. Puree to a smooth paste in a food processor.

5 Replace the pan over the heat, add the tomato sauce and chicken broth, and bring to a boil. Stir in the beef, chile paste, bay leaf, and cinnamon. Reduce the heat to low and simmer, uncovered, for 1 hour.

6 Add the oregano, cumin, and cayenne pepper. Let simmer, uncovered, for another hour. Add a little water or chicken broth if the chili becomes dry or overly thick.

7 Add salt and serve hot. Pass cornbread to crumble into individual bowls of chili, if desired.

EXTRA POINTS **Like many types of chili, this one tastes even better the next day, so feel free to make it ahead of time and reheat it on tailgate day.**

Smokin' Chicken Chili

Some people don't believe that anything containing chicken can actually be chili. But this recipe offers an alternative to heavier beef flavors, while still packing a lot of *taste*. Chipotles are smoked jalapeños. Look for the canned ones, in adobo sauce, in the Mexican food aisle of most supermarkets. Smoked paprika has a wonderful, *woody aroma* and taste that matches the chipotles; do not use regular paprika. Also, try Mexican oregano, if you can find it, to add authentic Mexican flavor to this dish. Finally, add more chipotles if you like to turn up the heat. SERVES 6

One 15-ounce can diced tomatoes, undrained
2 canned chipotle chiles in adobo sauce, plus
   2 teaspoons adobo sauce from can
4 tablespoons vegetable oil
2 pounds boneless chicken breasts, cut into
   1-inch cubes
1 cup chopped green bell peppers

1 cup chopped onions
1 teaspoon chopped garlic
One 15-ounce can black beans, rinsed and
   drained
1 teaspoon dried oregano (Mexican, if available)
1/2 teaspoon smoked paprika
Salt and freshly ground black pepper to taste

1   Place the tomatoes with their juice, the chipotles, and the adobo sauce in a food processor. Puree until mixture forms a smooth paste. Set aside.

2   Heat 2 tablespoons of the vegetable oil in a large saucepan or Dutch oven over medium heat, add the chicken, and sauté until the chicken is cooked throughout. Remove the chicken from the pan and set aside. Heat the remaining 2 tablespoons oil in the pan, add the green peppers, onions, and garlic, and cook until soft, about 5 minutes.

3   Return the chicken to the pan. Add the chipotle paste, black beans, oregano, paprika, and enough water to cover the ingredients. Bring to a boil, then reduce the heat and simmer, uncovered, for 45 minutes to 1 hour. Add salt and pepper. Serve hot.

EXTRA POINTS You can prepare the chili the night before and reheat it, or you can chop the chicken and vegetables the night before, refrigerate them in separate zipper-top plastic bags, and make the chili on site over a gas grill.

The Belle of the Gridiron

 OLE MISS COLLEGE FOOTBALL, OXFORD, MISSISSIPPI

*C*handeliers, silver chafing dishes, and lavish floral centerpieces adorn the tables at tailgates in The Grove at the University of Mississippi in Oxford. Sports magazines have called tailgating at The Grove (true fans call it "Groving") one of the best pregame experiences in the country. It is a unique slice of Southern football fandom at this 17,000-student school, where the Homecoming court and their escorts still don full-length ball gowns and tuxedos to stroll down the 50-yard line at halftime.

The Grove is a 10-acre area in the center of campus covered with huge, old oaks. On game days, the oaks share space with dozens of colorful tents, when as many as 10,000 fans crowd The Grove and its more family-friendly neighbor, The Circle. At one time, fans were allowed to actually park in The Grove, but damage to the sod and trees led officials to ban vehicles. This change has fueled a cottage industry. Out-of-town fans hire students for the season to set up their tents, which must be done sometimes as early as 9:00 P.M. the night before a noon game.

On game day, car horns blare "Dixie," the Ole Miss fight song, as fans pull rolling coolers and wagons full of food to their spaces. A Confederate uniform, complete with sword, adorns one tent. Young women in cocktail dresses and high heels walk by, waving to their friends. Some fans never leave the party in The Grove for the game, instead settling in with generators, satellite dishes, and TVs. For night games, fans simply connect electric chandeliers and keep on going.

The Grove isn't reserved just for fat-cat alumni. It is first-come, first-served, and designated spaces are set for unloading food and other accoutrements. Southern food abounds—fried chicken, pound cake, deviled eggs, cheese straws. And people visiting from tent to tent, sampling goodies, make The Grove seem like a small town. Technically, alcohol isn't allowed, but few take note, except when the guys in the tent next door swipe your liquor while you're at the game.

Main Courses

The main event means *big eats* and fan fuel. This is food for the land of the grilled and the home of the famished. The *spicy flavors* of pork ribs will please your crew, with a recipe that is easily pulled together. Or drop that cardboard bucket and make your own fabulous fried chicken, the classic tailgate treat. And there are plenty of recipes for the national nosh of sports fans—chicken wings. But really, what could beat the *ease and fun* of food on a stick? Grill up a batch of steak and vegetable skewers with spicy chimichurri sauce and feel the *action in your mouth* as well as on the field! Your friends might just forget about the game when you bring the *heat* with this food.

Wally's Game Chicken
with Sauce 70

Better-than-the-Bucket
Fried Chicken 72

Tropical Herb Chicken 74

Kim's PBF
Chicken Enchiladas 75

Rub 'Em Out Wings 76

New Year's Day
Slow Cooker Wings 77

Tandoori Touchdown
Wings with Mint-Mango
Chutney 78

Teriyaki Tip-Off Wings 80

Dynamite Wings 81

Fast Lane Fried Turkey 82

Thomas's Marinated
Gamecocks with Polenta 86

Double Play Spicy Beef 88

Sizzling Citrus
Grilled Steak 89

Grilled Steak and
Vegetable Skewers with
Chimichurri Sauce 90

Grilled Pork Tenderloin
with Dipping Sauces 92

Indoor/Outdoor Kiss-of-
Fire-and-Smoke Ribs 94

Linda's Super
Sauerkraut Stew 96

Thomas's Seared
Ginger Scallops 98

Jo's Hibachi Seafood Mix 99

Poached Salmon with
Garlic-Yogurt Sauce 100

Shrimp and
Couscous Salad 102

Norma's Cool
Veggie Pizza 104

Wally's Game Chicken with Sauce

North Carolina State University football fan Wally McKeel of Ahoskie, North Carolina, uses his family recipe for a chicken simmering sauce to make this *YUMMY* dish. "The meat will be falling off the bone," Wally says. Every football season, Wally designates one home tilt as his "chicken game." He feeds all comers, often more than 50 folks. The sauce should have a sweet-sour flavor. Taste it after stirring in all the ingredients and add more sugar, if desired, to your taste. SERVES 8

^{1}/$_2$ gallon cider vinegar

^{1}/$_2$ to ^{3}/$_4$ cup (1 to 1^1/$_2$ sticks) butter

One 24- to 28-ounce bottle ketchup, at room temperature

5 cups sugar

Juice of 2 lemons

3 tablespoons red pepper flakes

3 to 4 tablespoons hot pepper sauce, to taste

^{1}/$_2$ cup honey

Two 2^1/$_2$- to 3-pound whole chickens

1 Prepare a hot fire in a charcoal grill or preheat a gas grill.

2 Heat the vinegar in a large saucepan over low heat; do not boil. Add the butter and stir until melted. Add the ketchup, sugar, lemon juice, red pepper flakes, hot pepper sauce, and honey. Let simmer gently for 15 to 20 minutes while stirring, making sure all the ingredients are dissolved.

3 Using kitchen shears, cut each chicken in half down the center of the back and breast. Place the chicken halves on the grill and cook, turning as needed, until the chicken is almost done, about 30 minutes.

4 Transfer the chicken to large, disposable aluminum pans. Pour over enough sauce to cover the chicken, and cover the pans with foil. Place the pans back on the grill and cook for 30 to 40 minutes. Serve hot.

EXTRA POINTS The sauce will keep for up to 6 months, refrigerated in an airtight container. When packing for the tailgate, don't forget large, disposable aluminum pans for cooking the chicken in sauce on the grill. And if you're looking to serve sandwiches, you can shred the chicken and serve it on rolls with plenty of sauce.

Southern Fried Face-Off

Several hours before the Edmonton Oilers were set to play the Carolina Hurricanes for the 2006 Stanley Cup championship, the only ice in sight was in coolers, surrounding beverages. On a toasty June evening, fans wearing Hurricanes red handed bug-eyed Canadian visitors dressed in Oilers blue heaping plates of North Carolina–style pulled pork, hot off the grill, and bowls of boiled coastal shrimp.

Kids played street hockey in the parking lots surrounding the RBC Center. Rock bands blared. Tents with big-screen TVs were set up to accommodate those without tickets so that they could still see the game and share the experience.

When the Hurricanes arrived in 1997, the team had to build popularity from the ground up in this Southern city, where natives believed that ice was fit only for cooling their bourbon and branch water, not for playing a sport. Basketball, football, and NASCAR racing were the traditions. But most sports do have one thing in common: the tailgate. And 'Canes fans have brought a thriving tailgate scene to the National Hockey League.

Canadians who made the trek to Raleigh for the series, which ended with a Hurricanes victory in Game Seven, had never seen tailgating quite like this. For one thing, it's too cold in Edmonton, Alberta, for most of the hockey season for a lot of parking lot activity. (Edmonton has an average March high temperature of 34°F versus around 60°F in Raleigh, for example.) Many parking lots ban alcohol. And Edmonton's sports fans have more of a tradition of gathering in bars or at group events to watch games.

At 'Canes games, it's like a big block party feast that oozes warm Southern hospitality to all guests from the frozen North. At least, it does until the puck drops. And it looks like that Stanley Cup would hold an awful lot of fried chicken.

Better-than-the-Bucket Fried Chicken

Fried chicken is the *ultimate* tailgate food. But why pick up a fast-food bucket when homemade tastes so much better? The classic Southern method is to pan-fry rather than deep-fry the chicken. And, done right, the chicken isn't greasy. The secret is in the oil temperature, so use an instant-read thermometer to monitor the temperature. If you prepare the chicken the day before, it's as easy on game day as hitting the drive-through. SERVES 4 TO 6

1 cut-up chicken, or 8 of your favorite chicken parts (thighs, legs, or breasts)
1 quart buttermilk
Salt and freshly ground black pepper to taste

1/4 teaspoon cayenne pepper (optional)
1 tablespoon paprika (optional)
2 cups all-purpose flour
Oil or vegetable shortening for frying

1 Place the chicken parts in a large bowl and pour the buttermilk over them, making sure all the pieces are covered. Cover the bowl and refrigerate for at least 6 hours, or overnight.

2 When ready to cook, drain the chicken but do not rinse. Sprinkle lightly with salt and black pepper. If desired, combine the cayenne pepper and paprika, then sprinkle on the chicken pieces.

3 Place the flour in a large plastic bag. Add 3 or 4 pieces of chicken at a time, toss to coat, then shake off as much excess flour as possible when removing pieces from the bag.

4 In an electric frying pan or a heavy frying pan on the stove, pour in enough oil to come to a depth of about 2 inches and heat over medium-high heat to 350°F.

5 Gently place the chicken pieces in the pan, in batches if necessary to avoid crowding the pieces. Cover and cook for about 5 minutes, or until the undersides of the pieces just begin to brown. Then, uncover and cook for 4 to 5 more minutes, until the undersides are completely brown. Turn, cover, and repeat the process for the second side. (Or, if you prefer, you can leave the pan uncovered for the entire process, using a splatter screen to keep down the mess.) Adjust the heat as needed to keep the oil temperature at 325° to 350°F. Be sure that no pink juices run when the chicken is pricked with a fork and that the internal temperature is 180°F when checked with an instant-read thermometer.

6 Place the chicken on wire racks set over plates or newspapers to drain. When well-drained, place on platters and keep warm.

EXTRA POINTS **If cooking ahead for the tailgate, allow the chicken to cool completely, then wrap in heavy-duty aluminum foil and refrigerate. You can reheat it on the grill at the tailgate if you wish, but it's also delicious served cold.**

Tropical Herb Chicken

Moist, spicy, and beautiful, this chicken dish offers pro flavor that even a rookie cook can master. It's a *favorite* on the grill at my house. Use more hot sauce if you like the heat, and try combining two different hot sauces for extra flavor.

SERVES 6 TO 8

1¼ cups freshly squeezed orange juice
Juice of 2 limes
4 tablespoons fruity Caribbean-style hot pepper
   sauce
1 teaspoon ground mustard
2 tablespoons dried basil

2 tablespoons dried thyme
1 tablespoon dried marjoram
1 cup chopped fresh flat-leaf parsley
8 boneless, skinless chicken breast halves
   (4 to 5 pounds)

1　In a small bowl, combine the orange juice, lime juice, hot sauce, ground mustard, basil, thyme, and marjoram. Mix thoroughly, then stir in the parsley.

2　Place the chicken breasts in a large zipper-top plastic bag or a plastic container with a sealable lid. Pour in the orange juice mixture and distribute it evenly to completely coat the chicken breasts. Marinate in the refrigerator for 4 to 6 hours, turning occasionally.

3　Prepare a hot fire in a charcoal grill or preheat a gas grill.

4　Remove the chicken from the marinade and discard the marinade. Grill the chicken for 4 to 6 minutes per side, depending on the thickness of the breasts, until the chicken is done. Serve warm or at room temperature.

EXTRA POINTS Grill the chicken at the tailgate party. Or, you can cook the chicken the day before and refrigerate it to make great sandwiches at the tailgate with rolls or crusty French bread and a bit of Dijon mustard and mayo.

Kim's PBF Chicken Enchiladas

Kim Hughes of Wake Forest, North Carolina, became familiar with PBF when her son, Justin, began playing soccer for the University of North Carolina at Chapel Hill. It stands for *"Parents Bring Food,"* and it has become a tradition with the UNC men's soccer team after home games. Parents feed the players after the matches, which allows them a chance to get to know the players and each other. Coaches even use PBF as a recruiting tool. SERVES 20

4 whole boneless, skinless chicken breasts
3 tablespoons unsalted butter
1 medium-size yellow onion, chopped
One 1.25-ounce package taco seasoning
Salt and freshly ground black pepper to taste
One 8-ounce package cream cheese

1¾ cups shredded sharp cheddar cheese
1 cup shredded pepper Jack cheese
One 4-ounce can chopped green chiles
5 tablespoons prepared salsa verde
4 cups enchilada sauce
10 burrito-size flour tortillas

1   Preheat the oven to 350°F.

2   Cut the chicken breasts into 1½-inch-thick strips. Heat the butter in a large frying pan over medium heat. Add the chicken, onion, and taco seasoning, and sprinkle with salt and pepper. Cook, stirring, until the chicken is cooked through, about 10 minutes. Let cool, then shred or chop into small pieces. Set aside.

3   In a large bowl, combine the cream cheese, 1½ cups of the cheddar cheese, the pepper Jack cheese, chiles, salsa verde, and 1 cup of the enchilada sauce. Add the shredded chicken mixture and stir well.

4   Spoon about 5 tablespoons of the filling down the center of a tortilla, then roll it up and place it in a large baking dish, seam side down. Repeat with the remaining tortillas. Pour the remaining 3 cups of enchilada sauce over the enchiladas. Sprinkle with the remaining ¼ cup cheddar cheese. Cover the dish with aluminum foil and bake for 30 minutes. Remove the foil and bake for 10 more minutes, or until bubbly. Cut each enchilada in half and serve hot.

EXTRA POINTS You can prepare these at home earlier in the day and reheat them, covered with aluminum foil, in a hot oven or grill at the tailgate party.

Rub 'Em Out Wings

I threw these together for a tailgating trip for which I had been a bit rushed to get ready, and they came out *So good* that I decided to pass along the recipe to fellow tailgaters.   SERVES 6

12 whole chicken wings, split at joints and
    wing tips discarded
4 cups buttermilk
4 teaspoons vinegar-based hot pepper sauce,
    such as Tabasco, Crystal, or Vampfire
1 cup all-purpose flour
1 cup cornmeal

2 teaspoons onion powder
4 teaspoons garlic powder
2 teaspoons salt
2 teaspoons freshly ground black pepper
2 teaspoons cayenne pepper
Vegetable oil for frying

1   Place the wings in 2 large zipper-top plastic bags. In a large bowl, combine the buttermilk and hot sauce, and pour half into each bag. Seal the bags and shake gently so that all the wings are covered with the sauce. Refrigerate for about 2 hours.

2   Combine the flour and cornmeal on a large, shallow plate and set aside. Combine the onion powder, garlic powder, salt, black pepper, and cayenne pepper in a small bowl and set aside.

3   In a large, heavy frying pan, pour in enough oil to reach a depth of about 1 inch. Heat the oil over medium-high heat to 350°F.

4   Drain the wings in a colander but do not rinse. Rub each wing with the spice mixture, then dredge the wings in the flour-cornmeal mixture. Shake off any excess. Fry in batches, turning occasionally, until golden brown. Drain on a rack.

EXTRA POINTS You can prepare these wings the night before the tailgate, wrap them in heavy-duty aluminum foil, and refrigerate them. To reheat, place the wrapped wings over indirect heat on a grill or in a low oven. Or you can serve them at room temperature.

New Year's Day Slow Cooker Wings

It's the ultimate college football bowl game day—who wants to spend it in the kitchen? Pop these mustardy, *smoky* wings into your slow cooker and you'll never have to call time-out to cook or eat. SERVES 4

2 teaspoons chipotle hot sauce

$^1/_4$ cup coarse-grain mustard

$^1/_2$ teaspoon onion powder

$^1/_2$ teaspoon garlic powder

2 tablespoons chili sauce

$^1/_2$ teaspoon cider vinegar

8 whole chicken wings, split at joints and wing tips discarded

$^1/_4$ cup water

1   In a small bowl, stir together the hot sauce, mustard, onion powder, garlic powder, chili sauce, and cider vinegar.

2   Place the wings in the bottom of a $4^1/_2$-quart slow cooker. Pour in the water. Pour the sauce over the wings, stirring to coat well. Cook on HIGH for 2 hours. Serve hot or warm.

EXTRA POINTS You can make the sauce up to 2 days ahead and store it in an airtight container in the refrigerator.

Tandoori Touchdown Wings with Mint-Mango Chutney

These *Indian-inspired* treats will surprise your guests, because they're far from the average wings. Don't over-marinate the wings or the acid in the yogurt may cause the texture of the meat to be too soft. If you prefer, you can use nectarines instead of mangoes in the chutney. Garam masala is an Indian spice blend available in supermarkets or Indian markets. SERVES 8

16 whole chicken wings, split at joints and
   wing tips discarded
4 cups plain yogurt
2 teaspoons ground cinnamon
4 teaspoons garam masala
2 teaspoons ground coriander

1 teaspoon ground cloves
2 teaspoons ground turmeric
2 tablespoons chopped fresh ginger
4 cloves garlic, chopped
4 tablespoons vegetable oil
Mint-Mango Chutney (recipe follows)

1   Place the wings in 2 large zipper-top plastic bags. In a large bowl, stir together the yogurt, cinnamon, garam masala, coriander, cloves, turmeric, ginger, garlic, and vegetable oil, and pour half of the marinade into each bag. Seal the bags and shake gently to coat. Refrigerate for about 2 hours.

2   Prepare a medium fire in a charcoal grill or preheat a gas grill.

3   Remove the wings from the marinade (discard the marinade) and shake off any excess. Grill the wings, turning once halfway through, for about 30 minutes. Serve with Mint-Mango Chutney for dipping.

MINT-MANGO CHUTNEY   MAKES ABOUT 2 CUPS

2 cups chopped ripe mango
Juice of 1 large lime
$^1/_2$ teaspoon grated fresh ginger
1 teaspoon grated garlic

2 tablespoons finely chopped yellow or red onion
2 teaspoons chopped fresh mint leaves
$^1/_2$ teaspoon sugar

Stir all of the ingredients together in a medium-size bowl, cover, and chill for 2 to 3 hours to allow the flavors to blend. When ready to serve, stir well, mashing gently.

EXTRA POINTS Carry the wings in their marinade and the chutney to the tailgate in a cooler, and grill the wings on site.

Teriyaki Tip-Off Wings

This twist on teriyaki ups the fruity taste with pomegranate juice and a small amount of soy sauce. These wings will satisfy fans of flavor who don't favor heat. To minimize sticky cleanup, line the pan with aluminum foil before cooking. *Pomegranate juice* is becoming increasingly popular; you can find it in most larger grocery stores, as well as in Middle Eastern markets. If you can't find an unsweetened brand, a sweetened one will work, too, but taste the marinade before adding the sugar. SERVES 4

8 whole chicken wings, split at joints and
   wing tips discarded
3/4 cup unsweetened pomegranate juice
1/4 cup freshly squeezed orange juice
1/2 cup reduced-sodium soy sauce

1 teaspoon grated fresh ginger
2 cloves garlic, crushed
1/4 cup plus 2 tablespoons sugar
2 tablespoons vegetable oil

1   Place the wings in a large zipper-top plastic bag. In a medium-size bowl, combine the pomegranate juice, orange juice, soy sauce, ginger, garlic, sugar, and vegetable oil; stir well to dissolve the sugar. Pour the marinade into the bag. Seal and shake gently to coat. Refrigerate for at least 8 hours, or overnight.

2   Preheat the oven to 350°F.

3   Line a rimmed baking sheet with aluminum foil or spray it with nonstick cooking spray. Drain the wings well (discard the marinade) and place them on the baking sheet. Bake for 30 to 40 minutes, or until done. Serve warm.

EXTRA POINTS You can cook the wings the day before the tailgate, wrap them in heavy-duty aluminum foil, and refrigerate. To reheat, place in a 300°F oven or on the indirect-heat side of a grill.

Dynamite Wings

Handle with care! These wings use *habanero chiles*, the hottest chiles known to man. Be sure to wear rubber gloves when chopping habaneros. For extra heat, double the sauce recipe, reserve half in the refrigerator, then add the wings to the remaining sauce and marinate in the refrigerator for a couple of hours. Use the reserved sauce for basting during grilling. Yowza. SERVES 4

8 habanero chiles, stemmed and seeded
4 cloves garlic
1 medium-size yellow onion, cut into quarters
1/4 cup plus 1 teaspoon cider vinegar

1/2 teaspoon salt, plus more to taste
8 whole chicken wings, split at joints and wing
   tips discarded
Olive oil

1   Place the habaneros, garlic cloves, and onion in a food processor and pulse to finely chop. Remove to a medium-size bowl and stir in the vinegar and salt. Cover and refrigerate overnight to let the flavors blend.

2   Prepare a medium fire in a charcoal grill or preheat a gas grill.

3   Rub the wings with olive oil and sprinkle them lightly with salt. Coat liberally on both sides with the habanero mixture. Grill for 15 minutes, then turn, coat again with the habanero mixture, and grill for another 15 minutes. (Do not use the habanero mixture near the end of cooking.)

EXTRA POINTS You need to prepare the habanero mixture the day before the tailgate to allow the flavors to blend, but the wings are best prepared at the tailgate party.

Fast Lane Fried Turkey

Several years ago, I *deep-fried* my first Thanksgiving turkey, and it was so good that I've never gone back to roasting the bird. A deep-fried turkey is a *nearly perfect* food for famished sports fans. The cooking process offers entertainment, it's quick, and it's fried. What could be better? You'll find juicy birds sizzling in vats of hot oil everywhere fans gather, especially at NASCAR prerace camping. There are many flavors of injectable marinades available at the supermarket since fried turkey has become so popular; use your favorite. The marinade should be fairly thin and not contain any chunks that will clog the injector. You can find the fryer sets (which include injectors) needed for this recipe at hardware or home-improvement stores. SERVES 12 TO 15

4 to 5 gallons vegetable oil
One 12-pound whole turkey
1/3 to 1/2 cup Salt-Free Cajun Seasoning (page 57)
   or your favorite prepared rub

1 to 1 1/2 cups injectable marinade for fried
   turkeys

1   Place the pot on the fryer burner, then add the oil. Make sure the oil does not come more than about two-thirds of the way up the sides of the pot. Heat the oil to 390°F.

2   While the oil is heating, rinse the turkey inside and out, removing the package of giblets. Pat dry thoroughly with paper towels; any water will spatter when it hits the hot oil. When the turkey is dry, place it, legs down, on the rack provided with the cooker. Place the turkey on a cookie sheet and rub with the Cajun seasoning. Inject the marinade between the skin and meat in several areas, particularly around the breast. Use small amounts in many spots rather than a lot in one place.

3   Gently lower the turkey into the hot oil. If the oil does not completely cover the turkey, carefully add more until the bird is covered but the oil does not run over the sides of the pot.

4   Check the oil temperature frequently, and adjust the burner as necessary to maintain a temperature of 365°F during cooking. It will take 3 to 4 minutes per pound to cook the turkey, which means 35 to 45 minutes for a 12-pound bird. Check the turkey for doneness after about 35 minutes, or when the turkey has a crispy, brown skin. Remove the turkey from the oil, using the lifter hook provided, and test for doneness: an instant-read thermometer inserted into the thigh should register 180°F. If it doesn't, carefully put the turkey back in the oil and adjust the temperature as needed. Check again in 2 or 3 minutes. Be careful not to overcook the turkey.

5   Line a clean cookie sheet with several layers of newspaper or paper towels. When the turkey is done, remove it from the oil and place it, still on the vertical cooking rack, on the cookie sheet. Let drain and rest for at least 20 minutes before carving.

EXTRA POINTS **You can fry the turkey at home the day before the tailgate, but preparing it at the tailgate is a lot of fun!**

Don't Be a Real Turkey: Some Frying Advice

We've all seen the news footage on Thanksgiving of some fool setting his garage on fire with a turkey fryer. But with care and attention, frying a turkey is a safe process. Here are some things to remember.

- Only use a cooker setup specifically designed for frying turkeys. The equipment is widely available at hardware and home-improvement stores. The giant pot is also good for frying hush puppies, fish, or French fries for a crowd.

- Do not even consider frying a turkey indoors. This includes the garage or carport. An accident with the hot oil could quickly get out of control in an enclosed space.

- Place the cooker on a level surface free of flammable objects and away from foot traffic. The lawn is okay, but remove loose leaves or debris from the area surrounding the cooker. Keep children and pets out of the area.

- Before lighting up, check the propane lines to be sure they are functioning properly. The cooker should come with instructions on how to do this.

- When filling the pot with oil, remember that the turkey will displace some of the liquid. Ergo, if you fill the pot to the top and put in the turkey, the oil will spill over, catch on fire, and you'll be on the evening news. Start with the minimum amount of oil. Better to be a little short; you can add more oil after inserting the turkey. As your turkey-frying expertise grows, you'll know how much oil you need, or make notes for next time.

- Use a long fireplace match or long grill lighter to light the burner. Be sure to clip the thermometer to the side of the pot before lighting the burner to keep track of the oil temperature.

☛ Wear heat-resistant silicone oven mitts or welders' gloves when lowering the turkey into the hot oil, using the hook that comes with the fryer set. Also, wear eye protection and an old long-sleeved shirt (no loose clothing, though), because the oil may spatter. Lower the turkey slowly, not all at once.

☛ Do not leave the turkey unattended while it's cooking. If you need a beer, get someone to bring it to you. If you have to answer nature's call, bring in an assistant to watch the turkey. But never leave the area unmanned.

☛ Near the end of the cooking time, set up a removal rig: a heavy cookie sheet or other rimmed pan covered in newspaper or paper towels and placed on a sturdy table or other surface. Using the hook, lift the turkey from the oil and place it on the pan.

☛ Turn off the cooker and let the oil cool completely before attempting to move the pot or dispose of the oil. Strain it for reuse, if you fry turkeys a lot.

Thomas's Marinated Gamecocks with Polenta

Sure, they're really *Cornish game hens*. But when Thomas Lanford Jr.'s beloved University of Georgia Bulldogs play the University of South Carolina Gamecocks, this recipe is his way to sear the competition. Thomas says that polenta is actually quite easy to prepare at the outdoor tailgate.   SERVES 4

¼ cup honey

¼ cup soy sauce

2 tablespoons chopped garlic

2 tablespoons chopped fresh ginger

1 tablespoon freshly ground black pepper

1 cup water

2 Cornish game hens

Polenta (recipe follows)

1   Combine the honey, soy sauce, garlic, ginger, pepper, and water in a small saucepan. Cook over medium-low heat, stirring constantly, until completely blended. Allow to cool to room temperature.

2   Use sharp kitchen shears to cut the game hens in half down the center of the back and breast, and place in a large zipper-top plastic bag. Pour in the marinade, seal the bag, and refrigerate overnight.

3   When ready to cook, prepare a medium-low fire in a charcoal grill or preheat a gas grill.

4   Remove the hens from the marinade (discard the marinade) and grill until the juices run clear when the meat is pierced with a sharp knife, about 5 minutes per side. Serve over the polenta.

POLENTA

2 teaspoons butter or olive oil
1 teaspoon red pepper flakes
1 tablespoon minced garlic
1 cup finely ground cornmeal
1¹/₂ cups chicken broth
1¹/₂ cups water

Salt and freshly ground black pepper to taste
¹/₂ cup half-and-half
¹/₄ cup grated Parmesan cheese, or to taste
1 cup frozen green peas, thawed
2 tablespoons julienned fresh basil

1   Heat the butter in a large pot over medium-high heat. Add the red pepper flakes and garlic. Reduce the heat and cook until the garlic becomes opaque, about 30 seconds. Add the cornmeal, then whisk in the chicken broth and water. Add salt and pepper. Bring the mixture to a low boil, then reduce the heat to low and simmer, whisking occasionally, until the mixture thickens, about 20 minutes.

2   Whisk in the half-and-half. If the mixture is too thick, add a bit more chicken broth or water. Whisk in the Parmesan, peas, and basil. Taste and add more salt and pepper, if desired. Serve warm.

EXTRA POINTS Although you prepare the marinade and marinate the chicken the day before, make the rest of the dish at the tailgate.

Double Play Spicy Beef

This is one of those *great* dishes that can be dressed up for a pregame dinner or carried informally to a tailgate. What could be better—besides a big win? SERVES 6 TO 8

1½ teaspoons dried thyme

½ teaspoon dried marjoram

½ teaspoon garlic powder

¼ teaspoon plus a dash of cayenne pepper

½ teaspoon salt

2 teaspoons freshly ground black pepper

1 teaspoon paprika

2 pounds top sirloin steak or beef tenderloin

2 tablespoons olive oil

Juice of 1 lemon

1 tablespoon plus 1 teaspoon prepared horseradish

1 teaspoon chopped fresh chives

1 cup sour cream

¼ pound Parmesan cheese, thinly shaved

1   In a small bowl, combine the thyme, marjoram, garlic powder, ¼ teaspoon of the cayenne pepper, the salt, 1 teaspoon of the black pepper, and the paprika. Rub the mixture into the beef and let sit at room temperature for 20 minutes.

2   Heat the olive oil in a large nonstick frying pan over medium heat. When the pan is hot, cook the meat, turning to brown on all sides, until it reaches medium-rare. The amount of time this takes will depend on the thickness of the meat, but the temperature should read 140°F on an instant-read thermometer. Remove the meat to a cutting board and let it rest while you make the sauce.

3   In a small bowl, combine the lemon juice, horseradish, chives, sour cream, the remaining dash of cayenne pepper, and the remaining 1 teaspoon black pepper.

4   Slice the meat very thinly, place on a platter, pour the sauce over the top, and sprinkle with the shaved Parmesan. Serve warm or at room temperature.

EXTRA POINTS If you like, serve the slices of beef, topped with sauce and Parmesan, on bulkie rolls as sandwiches. Or to serve this as a hearty salad, toss salad greens and chopped tomatoes lightly with a red wine vinaigrette and top with slices of beef, the sauce, and Parmesan. No matter how you serve it, if you're transporting the dish to a tailgate, slice the beef on site to prevent it from drying out.

Sizzling Citrus Grilled Steak

Flank steak is great for grilling. It has lots of flavor, cooks quickly, and lends itself to so many uses. You can also use top sirloin here. For either cut, the secrets are to avoid overcooking the meat and to *slice it thinly*. Then eat it as is or tuck it into tortillas for fajitas. SERVES 6 TO 8

5 tablespoons soy sauce
$1/4$ cup freshly squeezed lemon juice
$1/4$ cup freshly squeezed lime juice
1 tablespoon sugar

3 cloves garlic, thinly sliced into ovals
$1/2$ large red onion, thinly sliced into rings
3 to 4 pounds flank steak

1   In a small bowl, combine the soy sauce, lemon juice, lime juice, and sugar. Stir until the sugar is dissolved. Stir in the garlic and onion.

2   Score the steak lightly on both sides with a sharp knife. Place in a large container or a large zipper-top plastic bag. Pour in the marinade and shake to coat the meat. Marinate in the refrigerator for at least 4 hours, or up to overnight.

3   Prepare a hot fire in a charcoal grill or preheat a gas grill.

4   Remove the meat and onions from the marinade (discard the marinade). Grill the meat and onions for about 5 minutes per side, or until the steak is rare to medium-rare, 135° to 145°F on an instant-read thermometer. Slice thinly and serve warm or at room temperature.

EXTRA POINTS You can serve this on rolls for sandwiches or make fajitas by wrapping the sliced beef and onions in tortillas and topping them with salsa and sour cream. If you like, throw some thinly sliced bell peppers on the grill as well.

Grilled Steak and Vegetable Skewers with Chimichurri Sauce

This quick recipe comes from Karen Adler and Judith Fertig's book *Weeknight Grilling with the BBQ Queens* (The Harvard Common Press, 2006), but it's also very weekend-tailgate friendly. For a *minimum of fuss*, you get to eat beef on a stick, saving the other hand for waving a giant foam finger. SERVES 4

1 pound boneless flank, hanger, or skirt steak
3 medium-size bell peppers in assorted colors (red, green, and yellow or orange), cored, seeded, and cut into wedges
1 large red onion, cut into 8 wedges

2 small yellow summer squash, ends trimmed and cut into 2-inch pieces
Chimichurri Sauce (recipe follows)

12 wooden skewers, soaked in water for at least 30 minutes prior to grilling

1   Lay the steak on a cutting board so that the grain of the flesh is horizontal. Cut the steak lengthwise into 8 strips. Place the strips in a baking dish and set aside. Place the bell peppers, onion, and squash in a large zipper-top plastic bag.

2   Prepare a medium-hot fire for direct cooking in your grill.

3   Pour $\frac{1}{3}$ cup of the chimichurri sauce over the steak, cover, and marinate for 15 minutes. Pour another $\frac{1}{3}$ cup over the vegetables in the bag, seal, and toss to coat. Set the remaining sauce aside until ready to serve.

4   Thread the steak strips lengthwise onto 8 skewers. Discard the remaining steak marinade. Thread the vegetables onto the remaining 4 skewers, any way you want.

5   Grill the vegetable skewers for 4 to 5 minutes per side, or until you have good grill marks. Grill the steak skewers, turning once with grill tongs, for 2 to 3 minutes per side for medium-rare or 4 to 5 minutes per side for medium. Serve hot or at room temperature, with the remaining chimichurri sauce on the side.

CHIMICHURRI SAUCE   MAKES ABOUT 1 CUP

$1/4$ cup chopped fresh Italian parsley

1 teaspoon dried oregano

3 cloves garlic, minced

$1/2$ teaspoon red pepper flakes

$1/2$ teaspoon salt

$1/2$ teaspoon freshly ground black pepper

$1/2$ cup olive oil

$1/4$ cup red wine vinegar

In a medium-size bowl, whisk together all the ingredients. Let sit for 10 minutes for the flavors to blend.

EXTRA POINTS This recipe is so quick and easy to prepare whether tailgating at home or on the road, but you could cut up the bell peppers and onions ahead of time, if you like.

Grilled Pork Tenderloin with Dipping Sauces

My good friends the BBQ Queens, AKA Karen Adler and Judith Fertig, believe that pork tenderloin or center-cut pork loin fillet is a great party food. Several tenderloins can go on the grill at once, and they *taste great* whether served hot, at room temperature, or chilled, so you can grill the pork the day before your tailgate. Be sure to purchase pork tenderloin or center-cut pork loin fillet, not pork loin roast. This recipe is from their book *The BBQ Queens' Big Book of Barbecue* (The Harvard Common Press, 2005). SERVES 8

4 pork tenderloins or 2 center-cut
    pork loin fillets (3¹/₂ to 4 pounds total)
2 tablespoons olive oil
Salt and freshly ground black pepper to taste

Cilantro-Peanut Dipping Sauce (recipe follows)
Chipotle Dipping Sauce (recipe follows)

1 Prepare a hot fire in a charcoal grill or preheat a gas grill.

2 Lightly coat the tenderloins with the olive oil and season with salt and pepper. Place directly over the fire. Grill the tenderloins for 2 to 3 minutes per side, turning a quarter turn at a time (grill center-cut pork loin fillets for 5 to 7 minutes per side, turning once), until an instant-read thermometer inserted into the thickest part registers 155°F and the meat is juicy and slightly pink in the center.

3 Remove to a cutting board and let rest for about 5 minutes, then cut on the diagonal into 1- to 2-inch-thick slices. Transfer to a platter and serve warm, at room temperature, or chilled, with the dipping sauces in bowls on the side.

CILANTRO-PEANUT DIPPING SAUCE MAKES ABOUT 1³/₄ CUPS

³/₄ cup crunchy peanut butter

¹/₄ cup soy sauce

¹/₄ cup rice vinegar

¹/₄ cup freshly squeezed lime juice

2 tablespoons jalapeño honey or regular honey

1 tablespoon toasted sesame oil

1 to 2 tablespoons chopped fresh cilantro

In a small bowl, combine all of the ingredients and stir until smooth. To make a thinner sauce, add a little more lime juice.

CHIPOTLE DIPPING SAUCE MAKES ABOUT 2 CUPS

2 cups chili sauce

1 canned chipotle chile in adobo sauce, plus
   1 teaspoon adobo sauce from can

1 tablespoon honey

1 tablespoon freshly squeezed lemon juice

¹/₂ teaspoon salt

In a food processor, combine all of the ingredients. Pulse 2 or 3 times to chop the chipotle and blend.

EXTRA POINTS The pork can be made ahead and served chilled at the tailgate or grilled on site. The dipping sauces can be made 1 day ahead of time. You can also serve the pork on sandwiches using crusty French bread or flatbread.

Indoor/Outdoor
Kiss-of-Fire-and-Smoke Ribs

Winning ribs are assured with this recipe adapted from *The BBQ Queens' Big Book of Barbecue* (The Harvard Common Press, 2005) by Karen Adler and Judith Fertig. Preparing the ribs ahead of time in the oven makes this a *great timesaver* for the tailgate. And the extra sauce will keep for several months in a covered container in the refrigerator. It's great on brisket or chicken as well as ribs.   SERVES 8

4 slabs baby back ribs
$^1\!/_2$ cup Ole Hickory Rub (recipe follows)
1 cup water-soaked hickory chips

2 cups BBQ Queens' Love Potion for the Swine
   (recipe follows)

1   Preheat the oven to 350°F. Line a baking sheet with heavy-duty aluminum foil.

2   Remove the membrane from the back of the ribs with a paring knife, heavy-duty tweezers, or needle-nose pliers. Sprinkle 2 tablespoons of the rub on the top side of each slab of ribs. Stack the ribs in 2 piles on the prepared baking sheet. Bake in the oven for about 2$^1\!/_2$ hours, rotating the ribs every 30 to 45 minutes. Remove the ribs from the oven.

3   Prepare a hot fire in a charcoal grill or preheat a gas grill. Add the hickory chips. Brush the "love potion" barbecue sauce on both sides of the ribs, and place the slabs on the grill. Turn and baste the ribs with additional sauce. Grill for about 15 minutes, until the sauce on the ribs has caramelized.

EXTRA POINTS The ribs can be baked up to 2 days ahead of the tailgate. Wrap them in foil and refrigerate, then grill them on site.

OLE HICKORY RUB   MAKES 2 CUPS

1/2 cup hickory salt

1/4 cup garlic powder or granulated garlic

1/4 cup onion powder

1/4 cup chili powder

3 tablespoons sweet Hungarian paprika

3 tablespoons packed light brown sugar

3 tablespoons ground mustard

1 1/2 tablespoons ground ginger

1 1/2 tablespoons red pepper flakes

Combine all the ingredients in a large glass jar with a tight-fitting lid. Secure the lid and shake to blend. The rub will keep in the cupboard for several months.

BBQ QUEENS' LOVE POTION FOR THE SWINE   MAKES 6 CUPS

One 24-ounce bottle ketchup

One 12-ounce bottle chili sauce

1/2 cup packed dark brown sugar

1/2 cup honey

1/2 cup cider vinegar

1/2 cup molasses

1/4 cup ground mustard

2 tablespoons red pepper flakes

1 tablespoon celery seed

1 tablespoon garlic salt

1 tablespoon Worcestershire sauce

1 tablespoon liquid smoke

1 teaspoon onion salt

1/4 cup water

In a large saucepan, combine all of the ingredients and simmer over medium-low heat for 45 to 60 minutes. After you pour the ketchup and chili sauce into the saucepan, turn the almost-empty bottles upside down to get the rest of the product out to add to the mixture. Use immediately, or pour into a covered container and refrigerate for up to several months.

Linda's Super Sauerkraut Stew

This recipe started a *standing tradition* for Linda Naylor of Chapel Hill, North Carolina. She found it in a magazine in 1988, and decided it would be a great dish to serve at a Super Bowl party. So, in 1989, she started having Super Bowl parties, and the recipe, with Linda's touches, has remained the star of the show. "One year I did fix something else and was politely requested by everyone to return to the usual," Linda says. Linda serves the stew with a few different hearty homemade breads, such as potato–caraway seed, onion-walnut, pumpernickel, or cheddar cheese–black pepper. **SERVES 20**

Six 29-ounce cans sauerkraut or
   10 pounds fresh bagged sauerkraut
4 cups water
1 pound bacon
4 large yellow onions, coarsely chopped
3 pounds beef chuck roast, cut into
   1-inch cubes

3 pounds pork loin, cut into 1-inch cubes
Salt and freshly ground black pepper to taste
2 pounds smoked garlic sausage, sliced
   1/2-inch thick
6 bay leaves
4 small yellow onions, cut into quarters

1   Preheat the oven to 350°F.

2   Rinse the sauerkraut with cold water and drain in a colander. Place the sauerkraut in a large pot with the water and bring to a boil. Simmer for 10 minutes and then drain. Put the sauerkraut into a large roasting pan.

3   In a large frying pan, fry the bacon over medium heat until crisp. Remove from the pan to drain, and set aside. Sauté the chopped onions in the bacon fat for about 4 minutes. Add the beef and pork and sauté until browned, 20 to 30 minutes. Season lightly with salt and pepper.

4 Add the contents of the frying pan, including the juices, to the roasting pan. Add half of the sliced sausage, all of the bay leaves, and the quartered onions to the roasting pan. Mix well. Scatter the remaining sausage on top. Cover and bake for 2 hours, then remove the cover and bake for another 30 minutes.

5 If the stew seems too juicy, thicken it with 4 teaspoons of flour rubbed into 1 table-spoon of butter. If it's too dry, add a little white wine or water. Serve hot or warm.

EXTRA POINTS This is a recipe for big eaters, but it freezes well. You can prepare it well in advance and freeze it all, make it 1 day ahead and freeze half for your next tailgate extravaganza, or serve it all and freeze any leftovers.

Thomas's Seared Ginger Scallops

University of Georgia fan Thomas Lanford Jr. of Atlanta, Georgia, has prepared this dish at tailgates for more than 30 *hungry* Bulldogs fans. During the summer, Thomas plans menus that run from appetizers to cocktails for every UGA game. Go, Dawgs! Sic 'em! Woof, woof, woof! SERVES 4

20 sea scallops
Salt and freshly ground black pepper to taste
2 teaspoons butter or olive oil, plus more
    if needed
2 tablespoons finely minced garlic
2 tablespoons finely minced fresh ginger

2 tablespoons orange zest
Juice of 1 orange
2 tablespoons orange-flavored liqueur,
    such as Grand Marnier
Julienned fresh basil for garnish
Rice pilaf for serving (optional)

1   Sprinkle both sides of the scallops with salt and pepper. Heat the butter in a large skillet over medium-high heat. Add the scallops and sear on both sides until just underdone. Remove the scallops from the pan and set aside on a plate; tent loosely with aluminum foil to keep warm.

2   Add more butter, if necessary, to coat the bottom of the pan. Over medium-high heat, quickly cook the garlic, ginger, and orange zest, stirring. Add the orange juice and reduce the heat to medium-low. Simmer gently until the sauce begins to thicken, 2 to 3 minutes.

3   Add the liqueur and, using a long-handled match or lighter, carefully light the mixture. Stand away from the pan, and tilt it slightly away from you, when you light it. When the flames die down, return the scallops to the pan and cook until the scallops are cooked through and coated with the sauce. Garnish with the basil.

4   If desired, serve over rice pilaf.

EXTRA POINTS This quick-cooking dish tastes best when made on site; I don't advise making it ahead of time. However, if you're serving it over rice pilaf, you can make the rice ahead of time.

Jo's Hibachi Seafood Mix

Fans of the University of Hawaii take the abundance of seafood on their island into account when tailgating. This recipe, which I adapted from Honolulu food writer Jo McGarry, traditionally calls for scallops in their shells, Manila clams, and *king crab legs*. Choy sum is a kind of Chinese cabbage that is related to bok choy; look for it in Asian markets. **SERVES 4**

¼ cup bottled clam juice mixed with ¼ cup water

½ pound choy sum or spinach

½ pound baby bok choy

2 pounds snapper fillets or other white-fleshed fish, cut into 3-ounce pieces

1 pound small clams in the shell

½ pound sea scallops

½ pound medium-size shrimp in the shell

Two 8-ounce lobster tails, meat removed from shell and cubed

½ cup (1 stick) butter, cut into pats

2 lemons

1 tablespoon chopped garlic

1 medium-size tomato, diced

¼ cup dry white wine

Dash of soy sauce

Salt and freshly ground black pepper to taste

1 Prepare a hot fire in a charcoal grill or preheat a gas grill.

2 Pour the clam juice–water mixture into a 9 x 13-inch disposable foil pan. Tear the choy sum and baby bok choy into individual leaves and place them on the bottom of the pan. Add the snapper, placing it near the center of the pan. Place the clams and scallops around the fish, and put the shrimp on top of the fish. Put the cubed lobster on top of the shrimp. Place the butter pats on top of all the seafood. Slice 1 lemon into thin circles and arrange on top of the butter. Sprinkle everything with the chopped garlic, diced tomato, white wine, and soy sauce. Sprinkle salt and black pepper lightly over the top.

3 Cover tightly with heavy-duty aluminum foil (you're steaming the seafood, so you want to keep all the steam inside) and place on the direct-heat side of the grill. Cook for 5 to 7 minutes (the foil will puff up after about 2 minutes), or until the fish flakes easily with a fork and the shellfish have opened slightly. To serve, slice the second lemon and place the slices on top for garnish.

EXTRA POINTS This steamed seafood dish is best prepared at the tailgate, just before serving.

Poached Salmon with Garlic-Yogurt Sauce

Who says tailgating can't have class? Impress your friends with this dish at a presteeplechase brunch, breakfast at Wimbledon party, or any summer tailgating event where lighter food is desired. It is so easy to prepare. Make sure the fillets are of an even thickness, with no thin areas that will overcook. The sauce was inspired by a recipe from a Turkish friend. She uses home-made yogurt, but Greek yogurt can re-create the tart flavor and thick texture. *Aleppo* is a medium-hot Turkish dried pepper that is used as a condiment. Look for it at Mediterranean markets or through spice catalogs. SERVES 6

3 pounds skin-on salmon fillets, about
 ¹/₂ inch thick
4 quarts water
4 tablespoons sherry vinegar
3 teaspoons salt

2 cups plain Greek yogurt
3 cloves garlic, crushed or finely chopped
1 teaspoon chopped fresh dill
2 teaspoons freshly squeezed lemon juice
¹/₂ teaspoon dried Aleppo pepper (optional)

1   Rub your fingers over the salmon and pull out any remaining pin bones. A small pair of clean needle-nose pliers or tweezers is good for this.

2   Bring the water to a boil in a saucepan or Dutch oven large enough to hold the salmon in one layer. When the water reaches boiling, stir in the vinegar and salt. Using a slotted spatula, gently lower in the fillets, skin side down. Reduce the heat to medium-low or so that the liquid remains at a very gentle simmer with bubbles rising slowly and occasionally.

3   Cook the salmon for 5 to 6 minutes or until medium-rare (still deep pink in the center when flaked with a fork). Carefully lift the fillets from the water with a slotted spatula and place them on a platter. Turn over and remove the skin with a fork or the spatula; discard the skin.

4 In a small bowl, combine the yogurt, garlic, dill, and lemon juice. Taste, then add a pinch of salt, if needed. Pour the sauce over the salmon, then sprinkle the Aleppo pepper, if using, on top of the sauce.

EXTRA POINTS If you like, you can prepare and refrigerate the salmon the night before the tailgate. Serve it chilled, with the sauce on the side. Do not prepare the sauce more than a few hours ahead of time, though, or the garlic flavor will become too strong. You can also wrap the chilled salmon and sauce in lavash bread for sandwiches.

Shrimp and Couscous Salad

You can adapt the dressing here to *your own taste*.
If you like more dressing on this main-dish salad, increase the proportions; if you prefer less mayo, cut back on it. Just be sure the couscous and shrimp are no longer warm before combining the ingredients, or they may wilt the vegetables or damage the dressing.   SERVES 8

One 10-ounce box plain instant couscous
1½ pounds medium-size shrimp
2 slices fresh lemon
1 green bell pepper, chopped
1 red bell pepper, chopped
4 green onions, sliced
One 12-ounce jar marinated artichoke hearts, drained and chopped

1¼ cups plain yogurt
¼ cup mayonnaise
3 to 4 tablespoons freshly squeezed lemon juice, to taste
Salt and freshly ground black pepper to taste
½ cup chopped fresh flat-leaf parsley

1   Prepare the couscous according to package directions. When done, place it in a large bowl and let cool to room temperature.

2   While the couscous cools, peel the shrimp. Place the lemon slices in a large pot with enough water to cover the shrimp and bring to a boil. Add the shrimp and cook for 1 to 2 minutes, or until the shrimp turn pink and are done. Drain and let cool; discard the lemon slices.

3   Add the green and red peppers, green onions, and artichoke hearts to the cooled couscous.

4   In a small bowl, combine the yogurt, mayonnaise, and lemon juice, adding enough lemon juice to give the dressing a pourable consistency. Add salt and black pepper.

5 Stir the cooled shrimp into the cooled couscous, along with the parsley. Add the dressing and toss to mix thoroughly. Refrigerate for about 4 hours before serving or overnight. Serve chilled.

EXTRA POINTS You can make and refrigerate this salad the night before your tailgate, or, if you prefer, you can cook the couscous and shrimp and chop the vegetables the day before and refrigerate, then assemble the salad on site. When serving, keep the salad chilled by nestling the salad container in a larger container or cooler filled with ice.

Norma's Cool Veggie Pizza

When mushers making the 1,000-mile trek across Alaska in the Iditarod sled dog race are hungry, the *Skwentna Sweeties* have hearty meals ready. Norma Delia is one of the Sweeties, a core group of women who prepare and organize food at one of the Iditarod checkpoints. She says this is a popular dish with the mushers.

MAKES 2 PIZZAS, APPROXIMATELY 14 INCHES EACH

Three 8-ounce packages refrigerated crescent rolls
Three 8-ounce packages cream cheese, softened
3¾ teaspoons mayonnaise
2½ cloves garlic, crushed
2½ teaspoons dried dillweed

Salt and freshly ground black pepper to taste
5 cups chopped assorted fresh raw vegetables of your choice: broccoli, cauliflower, peeled cucumber, green or red bell peppers, tomatoes, green onions, carrots, zucchini, yellow squash

1   Preheat the oven to 350°F.

2   Unroll each package of crescent roll dough and separate into 8 triangles. Use 12 triangles to make a circle, with the points in the center, on a baking stone or pizza pan. Press the seams together to seal. Repeat the process to make a second crust with the remaining 12 triangles. Bake for 12 to 15 minutes, or until golden brown. Cool completely.

3   In a medium-size bowl, combine the cream cheese, mayonnaise, garlic, dillweed, salt, and pepper; mix well. Spread half of the cream cheese mixture evenly over the top of each crust. Sprinkle half of the vegetables over the top of each pizza. Chill both pizzas for 30 minutes. Cut into wedges or squares and serve.

EXTRA POINTS You should prepare this dish right before serving, but you can chop the vegetables the night before and refrigerate them in zipper-top plastic bags.

Sweets from the Sweeties

THE IDITAROD TRAIL SLED DOG RACE, ANCHORAGE TO NOME, ALASKA

It's pretty cold in Alaska, and you'd think that would keep sports fans at home. No way. Hardy folks come out in force for the biggest sporting event in the state—the Iditarod Trail Sled Dog Race. The Iditarod kicks off on the first Saturday in March and runs for 1,049 miles across the wilderness over 10 to 17 days.

The race trail runs through the campus of Alaska Pacific University in Anchorage, and students have a tradition of coming out with goodies to cheer on the 85 or so teams. No matter that the high temperature at the start typically hovers in the low to mid 30s (and gets colder the farther north you go). With a lot of vegetarians on campus, sun-dried tomato basil veggie burgers are a favorite, along with chocolate chip cookies.

Fans gather all along the trail and hand snacks to the mushers as they go by. One Boy Scout troop manages to find a way to prepare hot lattes on the shore of a frozen lake and pass them to the mushers.

But no one can top the Skwentna Sweeties for feeding hungry fans, volunteers, and mushers. The Sweeties are a core group of women in the town of Skwentna, population 111, who spend weeks planning and preparing food for the mushers when they come through (and seeing to the canine comfort of each 16-dog team as well). Teams enjoy a feast that includes everything from stews to apple pies baked outdoors. The Sweeties end up feeding more than 100 people.

The Skwentna Sweeties, who have been honored for their work by the governor of Alaska, have been putting on the dog at the Iditarod for more than two decades.

Salads, Sides, Breakfast, and Brunch

Side dishes are sometimes neglected at the tailgate, overshadowed by the flashier ribs or grilled chicken. But *great sides* can lift a tailgate from the cellar to the championship. The tart flavor of marinated green beans or cucumber salad balances rich grilled food, and every winning team needs *killer cole slaw*. Besides, a few vegetables every now and then never hurt anyone.

Look here for breakfast and brunch dishes, too, suitable for *feasting* before those noon kickoffs or Sunday basketball tournaments.

Martha's Seven-Layer Salad 108

Crowd-Pleasing Marinated Green Beans 109

Mo's Mother's Coleslaw 110

Sheri's Chinese Salad 111

Bobbi's Spicy Slaw 112

Fresh Cucumber Salad 113

Kenny's Badadas 114

Kevin's Racin' Ears 116

Sheri's Carolina Caviar 117

Cool Classic Chicken Salad 119

Sweet Potato Ham Biscuits 120

Corny Cornbread 122

"Punkin" Mini-Muffins 123

Elizabeth's Baked Hush Puppies 124

Cousin Judy's Deviled Eggs 125

Michael's Sweet Potato Waffles 126

Big Game, Little Quiches 130

Jo Ann's Rockingham Gruel 131

Shelley's Girly Breakfast Casserole 132

Clota's Mountain Man Breakfast 133

Martha's Seven-Layer Salad

My friend and fellow University of North Carolina at Chapel Hill basketball fan, Martha Waggoner of Raleigh, North Carolina, brought this salad to an Atlantic Coast Conference Basketball Tournament brunch, and it has become a *staple*. She got the recipe from her mother and made a few changes of her own. Don't violate the eight-hour chilling rule or the penalty will be a less-tasty salad. SERVES 8

½ of a head of iceberg lettuce,
   coarsely chopped or shredded
1 cup chopped celery
1 cup chopped green bell peppers
One 17-ounce can small English green peas,
   drained

¼ cup chopped red onion, or more to your taste
1 cup mayonnaise (regular or low fat)
Grated Parmesan cheese to taste
4 slices bacon, cooked and crumbled

1   In a 2-quart clear glass bowl, layer the lettuce, celery, green peppers, peas, and red onion. Spread the mayonnaise evenly over the top without disturbing the layers. Top with Parmesan, then the crumbled bacon.

2   Cover tightly with plastic wrap and chill for at least 8 hours. Serve cold.

EXTRA POINTS You can prepare this salad the night before the game, but transport it carefully so as not to disturb the layers. Be sure to keep it chilled while serving, so store it in a cooler or nestle the bowl in another, larger bowl filled with ice.

Crowd-Pleasing Marinated Green Beans

My guests demand this salad for every sporting event, be it viewing basketball games on TV, tailgating at a football game, or gathering to watch a NASCAR race. It *travels well*, and it fills the void for those who believe that you should serve something resembling healthy food while watching a sporting event. Multiply the proportions to feed any size crowd of famished fans. SERVES 8

$^1\!/_2$ of a large red onion, thinly sliced

$^1\!/_3$ cup extra-virgin olive oil

$^1\!/_4$ cup Italian herb–flavored wine vinegar

Salt and freshly ground black pepper to taste

2 cloves garlic, crushed

2 pounds fresh green beans, ends trimmed

1   Bring a large pot of water to a boil. Place the sliced onions in a colander over the sink.

2   In a small bowl, stir together the oil, vinegar, salt, and pepper until combined. Stir in the garlic. Set aside.

3   When the water comes to a boil, add the green beans. Cover and cook for 5 to 10 minutes, or just until the beans are bright green; do not overcook. Pour the beans and hot water over the onions in the colander. Rinse under cold running water to cool down. Drain well for a few minutes.

4   Place the beans and onions in a large bowl or large zipper-top plastic bag. Pour the dressing in and mix with the vegetables. Chill for at least 4 hours or refrigerate overnight, stirring or shaking occasionally. Serve cold or at room temperature.

EXTRA POINTS You can use plain wine vinegar, but herb-flavored vinegar really makes this salad. It's easy to make your own: Combine 2 cups white wine vinegar with 1 cup fresh herbs (I use a combination of oregano and thyme, with a couple of cloves of garlic and a bay leaf thrown in). Pour into a clean glass jar and let sit away from direct light for 2 weeks. Taste it, and if it's not strong enough, let it sit for a few more days. Strain the vinegar into another clean glass jar and store it in the cupboard for up to 1 year.

Mo's Mother's Coleslaw

Consider mayonnaise-sodden slaw a personal foul? You'll love this *sweet-sour* recipe—there's not a dollop of mayo in sight. My friends Mo and Bobbi Courie (Duke fans) of Raleigh, North Carolina, brought it to a chili tasting during football season, and it was a great cooling complement to the spicy food. (I can see it next to some fried chicken, too.) SERVES 6 TO 8

1 small head green cabbage
1 green bell pepper, finely diced
$1/2$ teaspoon salt
$1/4$ teaspoon freshly ground black pepper

$1/2$ cup cider vinegar
$1/3$ cup sugar
2 tablespoons olive oil

1   Shred the cabbage using the shredding disc of a food processor, or finely shred by hand. Place in a large bowl and toss with the green pepper, salt, and black pepper.

2   In a small bowl, whisk together the cider vinegar, sugar, and olive oil. Stir the dressing into the cabbage mixture, cover, and refrigerate for several hours or overnight. Serve cold or at room temperature.

EXTRA POINTS You can prepare the slaw the night before the tailgate and refrigerate, or shred the cabbage and dice the pepper the night before and assemble the slaw in the morning. It is better made at least a few hours ahead, to give the dressing time to soak into the cabbage.

Sheri's Chinese Salad

This *great* salad from my friend Sheri Green combines Chinese flavors in an easy way. It's perfect for watching the 2008 Summer Olympics from Beijing—or any time you need an Asian-style side dish. SERVES 8 TO 10

1 head napa cabbage

6 green onions

One 15-ounce can mandarin oranges, drained

2 to 3 tablespoons vegetable oil

Two 3-ounce packages Oriental-flavor ramen noodles

$^1/_3$ cup shelled sunflower seeds

$^1/_3$ cup sesame seeds

$^1/_3$ cup slivered almonds

ASIAN DRESSING

$^3/_4$ cup vegetable oil

$^3/_4$ cup sugar

$^3/_4$ cup apple cider vinegar

2 packages of the seasoning mix from the ramen noodles

2 tablespoons soy sauce

2 tablespoons ground ginger

1 to 2 teaspoons red pepper flakes, to your taste

Dash of sesame oil

1 Chop the cabbage and green onions and put them in a large serving bowl. Stir in the mandarin oranges. Cover and refrigerate.

2 In a large skillet over medium heat, heat the vegetable oil. Lightly pound the noodles to break them up (set aside the seasoning packets), then add them to the skillet along with the sunflower seeds, sesame seeds, and almonds. Cook, stirring, until the mixture is lightly browned. Watch carefully, as the seeds and almonds brown quickly. Set the mixture aside to cool. Cover and refrigerate if not preparing the salad immediately.

3 To make the Asian Dressing, combine the vegetable oil, sugar, vinegar, seasoning mix, soy sauce, ginger, red pepper flakes, and sesame oil in a medium-size bowl. Cover and refrigerate if not serving immediately.

4 When ready to serve, add the noodle mixture and the dressing to the cabbage mixture and toss to combine thoroughly. Serve immediately.

EXTRA POINTS The 3 mixtures can be prepared the night before serving. However, do not combine them until you are ready to eat, because the noodles will become soggy. Add some chopped grilled chicken to make this a main-dish salad.

Bobbi's Spicy Slaw

My friend Bobbi Courie threw together this side dish for a chili-tasting party, and the *red cabbage* makes it truly a slaw of a different color. My taste-testers called this a slaw for people who don't like slaw. I reduced her suggested amount of celery seed; add more if you like that flavor. Bobbi adapted the recipe from one in *Not Afraid of Flavor: Recipes from Magnolia Grill* (University of North Carolina Press, 2000), by Ben and Karen Barker. SERVES 8 TO 10

1 medium-size head red cabbage, trimmed, quartered, and cored
1 fresh jalapeño chile, sliced (seeds optional)
2 cloves garlic
3 tablespoons cider vinegar, or more to taste
1 teaspoon mustard seed, crushed

1/2 teaspoon celery seed, crushed
2 teaspoons salt, or more to taste
Pinch of sugar, or more to taste
Pinch of cayenne pepper
1/4 cup vegetable oil
2 tablespoons sour cream

1   Finely shred the cabbage quarters in a food processor or by hand. Place in a large serving bowl.

2   Place the jalapeño in the bowl of a food processor or blender. Add the garlic, vinegar, mustard seed, and celery seed; pulse to puree. Add the salt, sugar, and cayenne. With the machine running, slowly drizzle in the vegetable oil. Add the sour cream and pulse to combine.

3   About 1 hour before serving, toss the cabbage with the dressing and refrigerate. Taste, then add more salt, sugar, and/or vinegar if desired. Serve cool or at room temperature.

EXTRA POINTS You can shred the cabbage and prepare the dressing up to 1 day ahead of time, but do not combine the two until 1 hour or so before serving time.

Fresh Cucumber Salad

This classic Southern salad provides *cooling* refreshment when the tailgate action is heating up. I like this salad tart, but add another tablespoon of sugar if you prefer a sweeter flavor. SERVES 6 TO 8

3 large cucumbers
1 medium-size sweet onion (such as Vidalia, OSO Sweet, or Texas 1050)
1½ cups rice vinegar
1 cup cider vinegar

3 tablespoons sugar
1 teaspoon salt
1 tablespoon celery seed
Freshly ground black pepper to taste

1   Peel and thinly slice the cucumbers. Thinly slice the onion. Place both in a large serving bowl.

2   In a small bowl, combine the rice vinegar, cider vinegar, sugar, salt, celery seed, and black pepper. Stir until the sugar is dissolved.

3   Pour the vinegar mixture over the cucumbers and onion and toss to combine. Cover and chill until ready to serve.

EXTRA POINTS This is another great do-ahead recipe. You can make it the morning of the tailgate or even at the tailgate, but this salad tastes even better if made the day before serving.

Kenny's Badadas

When preparing to go to a NASCAR race, Kenny Hussey of
Hanover, New Hampshire, and his friends Mark Kovac of
Lebanon, Pennsylvania, and Chris Broderick of Lebanon, New
Hampshire, spend weeks planning the food they'll eat while
camping in an RV for several days. Close to home at the
Loudon, New Hampshire, race, they enjoy cooking lobster and
clams. But Kenny's *Potatoes*, which are called "badadas"
for reasons now lost to history, are a must-have. This is a
flexible recipe—adjust the amounts to feed the number of fans
at your tailgate and to suit your own taste. SERVES 4 TO 6

3 to 4 pounds potatoes, peeled and cut into
   bite-size chunks or slices
1 green bell pepper, sliced into strips
1 red bell pepper, sliced into strips

1 yellow bell pepper, sliced into strips
1 teaspoon Salad Supreme seasoning blend or
   your favorite seasoning blend, or to taste
Salt and freshly ground black pepper to taste

1   Prepare a hot fire in a charcoal grill or preheat a gas grill.

2   Put the potatoes and peppers on a large sheet of aluminum foil (use heavy-duty foil or
a double layer of regular foil). Sprinkle on the Salad Supreme, salt, and pepper. Wrap the
mixture tightly in the foil.

3   Place the packet on the grill and cook until the potatoes are tender, 20 to 30 minutes,
shaking the packet occasionally. Serve hot or warm.

EXTRA POINTS You can slice the onions and peppers the night before the tailgate and refrigerate them in separate zipper-top plastic bags. Slice the potatoes
and assemble the packets just before cooking the dish.

Go Fast, Turn Left, Eat Big

*A*s a cold March night falls, clusters of hardy souls gather around wood fires at Thunder Valley, AKA Bristol Motor Speedway. Campers, RVs, and trucks toting tents pack campsites surrounding the towering oval in the mountains. These fans are already settled in because the real fun starts long before the green flag drops at the half-mile track.

Football fans may hang out for just a few hours. But NASCAR devotees are the ironmen and ironwomen of tailgating, spending up to a week cooking, visiting, and decorating. It amounts to a big family reunion. Bristol, which hosts two races a season, has a reputation as the friendliest track for campers, which seems well-founded. The long history of this track, built in 1961 and expanded to seat 160,000, brings out longtime lovers of this sport, which started in these hills with lead-footed, good old boys running moonshine.

The food for these speed fans needs to be big: ribs, burgers, and steaks. Some spend weeks planning menus. And the groups can be large; up to a dozen or more cooking and drinking together, plus new friends who drop by at the smell of good food or the sound of a pop-top. Generators buzz and satellite dishes pick up signals for big-screen TVs, which many place in their RV luggage areas, allowing alfresco viewing.

Many are partisan fans, of course. You'll see flags with driver numbers, and folding chairs and even decorative lights in driver colors. But a lot of people come for the tailgate, fun, and good eating, with the race just as an excuse. "You come for the race, but you stay for the food and friends," says fan Tim Beck of Archbold, Ohio.

Kevin's Racin' Ears

There usually ends up being a crowd of 12 to 14 hungry fans around when Kevin Csernyik of Talmadge, Ohio, and his buddies head to a NASCAR event. Kevin's version of classic *Corn* roasted in the husk keeps the gang going. Multiply the ingredients to feed any number of gear heads. Make sure to use the pump variety of butter-flavored cooking spray that's found in the refrigerated case at the supermarket, not the aerosol kind. SERVES 10

10 ears fresh corn, still in the husks
Refrigerated butter-flavored cooking spray

2½ to 3 teaspoons garlic salt

1   Prepare a medium-hot fire in a charcoal grill or preheat a gas grill.

2   Submerge the ears of corn, still in the husks, in cold water for about 30 minutes. Drain, then gently peel back the husks without removing them. Using a small brush, remove as much of the corn silk as possible from the corn. Pat the corn dry with paper towels.

3   Spray each ear of corn with the cooking spray, then sprinkle about ¼ teaspoon garlic salt on each ear. Rewrap the husks around the corn, then wrap each ear in aluminum foil. Place on the indirect side of the heat and grill for 30 to 45 minutes, turning occasionally. Remove the foil, strip off the husks, and serve hot or warm.

EXTRA POINTS You can soak and clean the corn the day before the tailgate; rewrap the husks around the ears and refrigerate overnight. If you can't find corn still in the husks, wrap the cleaned corn directly in the aluminum foil and skip the soaking. The corn may take less time to cook this way, so check it after about 15 minutes. A touch of chili powder would add a Southwestern flavor to the corn.

Sheri's Carolina Caviar

My friend Sheri Green of Raleigh, North Carolina, brought this *salad* to a party for the 2006 Winter Olympics opening ceremonies, where guests offered fashion commentary on the athletes' uniforms. Despite some spirited debates about the clothes, there were no bad reviews for this dish. Sheri uses Girard's Olde Venice Italian Salad Dressing, but use your own favorite. Serve with crackers or French bread. SERVES 6

Two 15-ounce cans black-eyed peas, rinsed and drained

One 10-ounce can diced tomatoes with green chiles, undrained

$1/4$ cup chopped black olives

$1/4$ cup chopped green olives

$1 1/2$ to 2 tablespoons onion flakes, to your taste

$1/4$ to $1/2$ cup Italian salad dressing, to your taste

1   In a large bowl, combine the black-eyed peas, tomatoes, black olives, and green olives. Stir in $1 1/2$ tablespoons of the onion flakes and $1/4$ cup of the salad dressing. Taste, then add more onion flakes and/or salad dressing, if desired.

2   Cover and chill for several hours. Serve chilled or at room temperature.

EXTRA POINTS You can make and refrigerate this salad the night before the tailgate or prepare it on the morning of the tailgate. Just be sure to give it a little time for the flavors to blend before serving.

The Land of the Brat

The smoke rising from dozens of grills surrounding legendary Lambeau Field in Green Bay, Wisconsin, carries not the aroma of namby-pamby boneless chicken breasts, but the manly, pungent whiff of meaty pork links.

That heavenly scent is the smell of bratwurst—to true fans, simply "brats."

Brats (rhymes with "lots") are practically the state sports food of Wisconsin, celebrated in festivals and subject to more cooking and serving rules than a Victorian banquet. First of all, even though brats are cooked on a grill, the term for the event is a "brat fry" or simply "fry out," as in, "Come over to watch the game Sunday, we're gonna fry out." One need not say that brats are the star.

Brats go straight onto the grill. Turn them with tongs; don't stab at them with a big old fork, unless you want all the juices to run out.

Cooking for a crowd or waiting for kickoff? Pros keep grilled brats warm in a simmering combination of two or three cans of beer (often called "bratwash"), a sliced onion, and a stick of butter. No one ever said this was low-calorie cuisine.

Brats are never served in plebeian hot dog buns. Rather, they are cradled in hard rolls similar to kaiser or Bavarian semmel rolls. Never should yellow mustard touch a brat; it's German-style brown mustard only. Dijon mustard is acceptable, in a pinch. Then, add chopped grilled or raw onion. Ketchup and sauerkraut are controversial additions, and some people butter the rolls before applying the brats.

In Sheboygan, the self-proclaimed brat capital of the world and home to the Jaycees' Bratwurst Day on the first Saturday in August, asking for sauerkraut denotes a brat rookie. There, fans like a "double with the works": Two grilled brats on a Sheboygan hard roll with pickles, ketchup, onions, and brown mustard.

Cool Classic Chicken Salad

It seems that the simplest foods are some of the most difficult to prepare well. Chicken salad is one of those. Over time, it's been gussied up with grapes and other chunky ingredients for eating with a fork. But chicken salad for tailgating needs to be *smooth* enough to make a great sandwich, without having chunks drop out while you're eating it. Serve this chicken salad on regular sandwich bread or French bread at a fancy Kentucky Derby party, before a big football game, or while watching U.S. Open tennis—it goes anywhere. SERVES 6

2 pounds boneless chicken breasts
1 sprig fresh thyme (optional)
$3/4$ cup finely chopped celery
$1/4$ cup finely chopped onion

$1/2$ cup finely chopped pecans
$1^1/4$ cups mayonnaise
Salt and freshly ground black pepper to taste

1   Place the chicken breasts and the thyme, if using, in a large saucepan and put in enough cold water to cover by 2 or 3 inches. Bring to a boil, then reduce the heat to a simmer and cook for 30 minutes, or until the chicken is fully cooked.

2   Discard the thyme, remove the chicken to a platter, and let cool. When cool enough to handle, shred the chicken and place it in a large bowl.

3   Add the celery, onion, pecans, and mayonnaise, and mix well until combined. Add the salt and black pepper. Cover and chill until cold.

EXTRA POINTS You can cook and shred the chicken and chop the celery, onions, and pecans the day before the tailgate, refrigerating everything in zipper-top plastic bags, and then toss the salad on site. Or you can prepare and refrigerate the whole dish the day before the tailgate. When serving, keep the salad container nestled within a larger container filled with ice to keep the salad cold.

Sweet Potato Ham Biscuits

Ham biscuits are on the table at every Southern tailgate, family reunion, or brunch. Adding sweet potatoes to the biscuits adds a contrast to the salty ham and offers a *beautiful color* to your spread. If you can find biscuit-slice country ham or regular thin-sliced country ham, buy that rather than a whole small ham.   MAKES ABOUT 15 BISCUITS

2 cups all-purpose flour
2 teaspoons baking powder
1 teaspoon baking soda
1 tablespoon sugar
$1/4$ teaspoon salt
$1/4$ teaspoon ground cinnamon

$1/4$ cup ($1/2$ stick) cold unsalted butter,
   cut into cubes
$1^1/2$ cups cooked, mashed sweet potatoes,
   cooled to room temperature
1 cup buttermilk
10 ounces country ham

1   Preheat the oven to 450°F. Spray a rimmed baking sheet with nonstick cooking spray.

2   In a large bowl, combine the flour, baking powder, baking soda, sugar, salt, and cinnamon. Using a pastry blender, cut in the butter cubes until the mixture resembles coarse cornmeal.

3   In a medium-size bowl, combine the sweet potatoes and buttermilk. Stir the potato-buttermilk mixture into the flour mixture, stirring just until the dough begins to come together. Add a little more buttermilk if the dough is dry and not holding together. The dough should be very moist.

4   Lightly flour your hands and a clean work surface. Turn the dough out onto the floured surface and knead lightly to combine; do not use too much flour (not more than about $1/2$ cup additional flour). Press or roll out the dough to a $1/2$-inch thickness. Cut with a 2- or $2^1/2$-inch biscuit or round cookie cutter. Place the biscuits on the baking sheet, very close together but not touching, about $1/2$ inch apart. Bake for 10 to 12 minutes or until lightly brown; watch carefully near the end to avoid burning. Remove the biscuits to a rack and let cool.

5   Prepare the ham according to the package directions and drain well. Slice thinly, if necessary.

6   To serve, slice the biscuits in half, cut the ham slices to fit the biscuits, and insert the ham into the middle of each biscuit.

EXTRA POINTS The biscuits can be made several hours ahead or 1 day before the tailgate. If you don't want to use ham, make the biscuits into a sweet breakfast treat: Combine 2 tablespoons unsalted butter with $1/4$ to $1/2$ cup orange juice in a small saucepan and heat until the butter melts and mixes with the juice. Brush the biscuits with the mixture before baking.

Corny Cornbread

This *fluffy* cornbread is a longtime favorite at my house with chili, soup, or even meatloaf. Use either yellow or white cornmeal, it's your preference, but do look for good stone-ground meal. I bake this in my mama's cast-iron frying pan, which she received as a wedding gift in . . . well, let's just say it was quite some time ago. Baking cornbread in cast iron makes a great crunchy crust; try it. If you don't have a cast-iron frying pan, use a conventional pie pan.   SERVES 8

5 tablespoons unsalted butter, melted
1 cup all-purpose flour
1 cup stone-ground cornmeal
$^1/_2$ teaspoon salt
2 teaspoons baking powder

$^1/_2$ teaspoon baking soda
1 cup buttermilk
One 8.25-ounce can cream-style corn
1 tablespoon sugar
1 large egg

1   Preheat the oven to 350°F. Place 2 tablespoons of the melted butter in a cast-iron frying pan or pie plate and swirl to coat the pan with the butter. Set aside.

2   Combine the flour, cornmeal, salt, baking powder, and baking soda in a large bowl. In another large bowl, combine the remaining 3 tablespoons melted butter, the buttermilk, creamed corn, sugar, and egg, and blend until well combined. Pour the wet ingredients into the dry ingredients and stir quickly until just combined and no lumps remain.

3   Pour the batter into the pan. Bake for 30 to 40 minutes, or until a toothpick or wooden skewer inserted into the center comes out clean. Let cool for a few minutes, then serve warm, right from the pan.

EXTRA POINTS You can make this ahead, but nothing beats eating it fresh and hot right out of the pan!

"Punkin" Mini-Muffins

Andy Griffith was a North Carolina native and his classic 1953 comedy routine, "What It Was Was Football," inspired these *sweet-spicy treats* made with canned pumpkin. Make sure to use pumpkin puree and not pumpkin pie filling, which has added ingredients. Eat them while you watch teams play with the "funny-looking little punkin." My taste-testers loved the moistness of these gems. MAKES ABOUT 5 DOZEN MINI-MUFFINS

3¹/₂ cups all-purpose flour

2 teaspoons baking soda

1¹/₂ teaspoons salt

2¹/₈ teaspoons ground cinnamon

¹/₂ teaspoon ground ginger

¹/₈ teaspoon ground cloves

1 teaspoon ground nutmeg

1¹/₄ cups sugar

1 cup vegetable oil

4 large eggs

One 15-ounce can pumpkin puree

²/₃ cup water

¹/₂ teaspoon pure vanilla extract

1   Preheat the oven to 350°F. Coat mini-muffin tins with nonstick cooking spray. (You may need to bake in batches.)

2   In a large bowl, sift together the flour, baking soda, salt, cinnamon, ginger, cloves, and nutmeg. In a medium-size bowl, combine the sugar, vegetable oil, eggs, pumpkin puree, water, and vanilla extract. Stir with a whisk to blend well, or use an electric mixer. Pour the wet ingredients into the dry ingredients and stir until combined and smooth and no lumps remain.

3   Spoon about 1 heaping tablespoon of batter into each muffin well, so that the wells are about two-thirds full with batter. Bake for 15 minutes, until a toothpick inserted into the center of a muffin comes out clean. Cool in the tins for 15 minutes, then remove.

EXTRA POINTS These muffins freeze beautifully. Cool them completely, then seal in zipper-top plastic freezer bags. You can also make loaves, if you prefer. Pour the batter into two 5 x 9-inch loaf pans and bake for 45 minutes to 1 hour.

Elizabeth's Baked Hush Puppies

If you want to keep light on your feet and ready for action, saving a few fat grams by using this *no-fry recipe* isn't a bad idea. And hush puppies are another round food, like my beloved sausage balls (page 30), which are perfect for expressing oneself after a bad ref call. My friend Elizabeth Swaringen of Pittsboro, North Carolina, adapted this recipe from one in *Low-Fat Soul* (Ballantine Publishing Group, 1996), by Jonell Nash. MAKES 24 HUSH PUPPIES

1 cup yellow cornmeal
$^{1}/_{2}$ cup all-purpose flour
$1^{1}/_{2}$ teaspoons baking powder
1 teaspoon sugar
$^{1}/_{2}$ teaspoon salt
1 teaspoon garlic powder
$^{1}/_{2}$ teaspoon cayenne pepper

2 egg whites, beaten
$^{1}/_{2}$ cup skim milk
2 tablespoons vegetable oil
$^{1}/_{2}$ cup finely chopped green onions
1 teaspoon finely chopped fresh jalapeño chiles, or more to taste
Cocktail sauce for serving (optional)

1 Preheat the oven to 425°F. Coat mini-muffin tins with nonstick cooking spray (you need 24 muffin wells).

2 In a large bowl, combine the cornmeal, flour, baking powder, sugar, salt, garlic powder, and cayenne pepper. Stir well. In a medium-size bowl, combine the egg whites, milk, and vegetable oil. Stir well. Add the egg mixture to the cornmeal mixture and combine until just blended. Stir in the green onions and jalapeños.

3 Spoon about 1 tablespoon of batter into each muffin well. Bake until the hush puppies are golden brown, 15 to 20 minutes. Let cool, then pop them out of the wells. Serve warm with cocktail sauce, if desired.

EXTRA POINTS You can bake these 1 day ahead and reheat them at the tailgate, wrapped in aluminum foil and placed on a corner of the grill.

Cousin Judy's Deviled Eggs

My cousin Judy Ross makes these *smooth*, tart deviled eggs, which fit in nicely at a family reunion or while watching a NASCAR race. This recipe is from my book *Deviled Eggs: 50 Recipes from Simple to Sassy* (The Harvard Common Press, 2004). **MAKES 12 DEVILED EGGS**

6 hard-cooked eggs, peeled, cut in half, and yolks mashed in a bowl

2 tablespoons mayonnaise

2 teaspoons yellow mustard

2 teaspoons Worcestershire sauce

3/4 teaspoon Old Bay seasoning

1 teaspoon distilled white or cider vinegar

1/4 teaspoon freshly ground black pepper

Salt to taste

Paprika for garnish

1   In a medium-size bowl, combine the thoroughly mashed egg yolks with the mayonnaise and mustard. Stir in the Worcestershire sauce, Old Bay, vinegar, and pepper. Because of the Worcestershire and Old Bay, the filling is pretty salty already, but taste and add more salt if you wish.

2   Fill the egg whites evenly with the mixture and garnish each egg half with a sprinkle of paprika. Serve cold.

EXTRA POINTS To avoid last-minute preparations, these deviled eggs can be made the day before the game or race. In fact, they taste better if the flavors have had time to combine. Cover with plastic wrap and refrigerate. If you don't have a deviled-egg plate, just cover a regular plate or sturdy paper plate with curly parsley and nestle the egg halves in it for a great, no-slip presentation.

Michael's Sweet Potato Waffles

At an *elegant* brunch before the Brookhill Steeplechase in Clayton, North Carolina, Michael Martin prepares sweet potato waffles, which I've adapted here. Michael started out with a recipe he found on the Food Network Web site, but modified it to reduce the fat and calories. Although this version calls for brown sugar, Michael uses a brown sugar substitute for baking (such as Splenda), so feel free to use that if you wish. The optional whipped cream adds a touch of *decadence*. Serve these waffles during those early-morning satellite-dish soccer games.   MAKES 5 TO 6 WAFFLES, DEPENDING ON THE SIZE OF YOUR WAFFLE MAKER

3 medium-size sweet potatoes
1/2 cup egg substitute or egg whites
1 tablespoon light buttery spread (such as
   Smart Balance Light), at room temperature
1 cup fat-free buttermilk
2 tablespoons light brown sugar
1 tablespoon orange zest

2 cups reduced-fat baking mix (such as Reduced-
   Fat Bisquick)

GARNISHES
Chopped toasted pecans
Maple syrup
Whipped cream (optional)

1   Peel the sweet potatoes and cut them into cubes. Place in a steamer over boiling water and steam for 20 minutes, or until you can pierce the cubes easily with a fork. Remove and allow to cool slightly, then whip the potatoes with an electric mixer until smooth.

2   Measure 1 1/2 packed cups of the sweet potatoes into a large bowl, reserving any leftovers for another use. Add the egg substitute, buttery spread, buttermilk, brown sugar, and orange zest to the bowl. Mix with a wooden spoon or with a mixer until smooth and thoroughly blended.

3   Stir in the baking mix. Mix until just combined, being careful not to overmix. Let the batter rest for 5 minutes.

4 Preheat a waffle maker. Pour in about ¾ cup of the batter, or the amount your waffle maker requires, and cook until done. Repeat until all the batter is used up.

5 Serve the waffles hot or warm with chopped toasted pecans, maple syrup, and/or whipped cream, if desired.

EXTRA POINTS You can prepare these waffles up to 3 days ahead of time. Cool them completely and freeze them in zipper-top plastic bags or airtight containers. When ready to serve, warm them in a 200°F oven. To toast the pecans and make them more flavorful, toss them in a dry frying pan over medium heat just until fragrant. Do not allow them to brown.

Oh, There's a Horse Race?

*E*ven before the Elvis impersonator arrived at the faux-casino tailgate, it was obvious that watching horses run through a field was not the main point of the Brookhill Steeplechase.

The man leaning on a rail as he watched the hat contest said it all, with a sip of his drink and a grin: "Yeah, I heard there was a horse race, too."

On the first Saturday in May, the same day as the Kentucky Derby, the Raleigh, North Carolina, Jaycees organize this race/eating fest/cocktail party as a fundraiser. Corporations use it for schmoozing clients. But average tailgate fans take it as an opportunity to express themselves in ways from elegant to wacky.

A group of women in little black dresses erected a tombstone-shaped sign proclaiming themselves the Golf Widows of Brookhill and decorated it with roses spray-painted black. Nearby, a white picket fence surrounded another tailgate area, which had horse-shaped balloons floating in the breeze. An elegant group, with white damask tablecloths on their round tables, set up a machine to shoot bubbles into the blue sky. An antiques dealer brought in a lawn jockey, a bronze horse statue, and an antique sideboard-bar for his tent.

But the tailgate casino was the craziest. It had cigarette girls, in short skirts and red sequined hats, walking the grounds with candy in their trays. The group

decorated a pickup truck with paper bells and flowers and labeled it "Brookhill Wedding Chapel." And then there was Elvis, of course. Who doesn't love Elvis at a horse race?

While waiting for grills to heat up or for secret sauces to work their magic on slabs of ribs, folks sipped beverages in the shade, played bocce ball or horseshoes (naturally), or strolled around to visit. Some watched the hat contest, which was won by a little girl with a two-foot pink stuffed unicorn attached to a very large hat. A "Spirit of Brookhill" award went to an appropriately themed chapeau adorned with swizzle sticks, margarita glasses, and tonic water bottles.

The race has been held for more than a decade in rolling fields near the fast-growing Raleigh, North Carolina, area. But that growth is now consuming Brookhill, as has happened with other steeplechases around the country. The farmland on which the event is held has been sold to developers, and the future of the steeplechase is uncertain. Knowing that doesn't stop the party—it just makes it sweeter.

Big Game, Little Quiches

When I host brunch for the Atlantic Coast Conference Basketball Tournament finals, quiche is always on the menu. These *bite-size* versions let folks eat with their fingers so they don't miss any of the action. Be sure to buy refrigerated pie crusts, as the frozen kind won't work in this recipe. **MAKES ABOUT 45 QUICHES**

2 prepared refrigerated 9-inch pie crusts
3 large eggs
1¹/₂ cups half-and-half
¹/₄ teaspoon freshly ground black pepper
¹/₂ teaspoon salt
¹/₂ teaspoon ground mustard

1 tablespoon finely chopped fresh flat-leaf parsley
1¹/₂ teaspoons finely chopped fresh dill
1¹/₂ teaspoons finely chopped fresh chives
About 2 tablespoons grated Parmesan cheese

1   Coat mini-muffin tins with nonstick cooking spray (you need 45 muffin wells). Let the pie crusts come to room temperature, then gently roll them out over the mini-muffin pans. Press the pie crust gently into the pans, trimming away excess with a sharp knife. Combine the excess crust and re-roll to use it all. Prick the shells with a fork and bake according to the package directions for a regular-size pie crust.

2   While the crusts are cooking, beat the eggs lightly in a large bowl. Whisk in the half-and-half, black pepper, salt, and ground mustard. Set aside. In a small bowl, combine the parsley, dill, and chives. Set aside.

3   When the crusts are done, let cool slightly. Set the oven temperature to 350°F.

4   Put a good pinch (about ¹/₈ teaspoon) of Parmesan in the bottom of each crust. Top with a good pinch (about ¹/₈ teaspoon) of the herb mixture. Fill each crust with some egg mixture (a small cup with a pour spout is good for this).

5   Bake for 30 minutes, or until the filling is firm. Serve warm or at room temperature.

EXTRA POINTS Need to save time? Omit the pie crusts and make crustless mini-quiches. Be sure to spray the muffin tins thoroughly to prevent sticking. Whether crustless or with crusts, the quiches can be wrapped in foil and refrigerated overnight after baking. Warm them, still wrapped, in a 200°F oven for about 15 minutes, or put them on a corner of the grill to reheat, before serving.

Jo Ann's Rockingham Gruel

This is Jo Ann Hlavac's favorite tailgating breakfast recipe.
Jo Ann is Race Mama of the awesome NASCAR fan Web site
www.laidbackracing.com, and this recipe was on the menu when
her group was attending races at North Carolina Speedway
in Rockingham, North Carolina. "We call it Rockingham
Gruel because we always ate it at The Rock," Jo Ann says.
"It was always cold at The Rock and we needed something
belly-warming to get us through the race." SERVES 4

¹/₃ to ¹/₂ pound bacon or sausage
6 large eggs
2 cups water
Four 1-ounce packages instant grits

Shredded cheddar cheese (optional)
Dash of freshly ground black pepper
Dash of hot pepper sauce
Salt to taste

1 Cut the bacon slices in half or crumble the sausage. In a large frying pan over medium heat, cook the bacon until crispy or the sausage until done. Drain well on paper towels. Add the eggs to the pan and scramble. Return the bacon to the pan and stir to combine.

2 Bring the water to a boil in a large saucepan, then add the grits and the eggs-and-meat mixture. Cover, reduce the heat to low, and cook for 5 minutes. Stir in the cheese, if using, after 3 minutes of cooking.

3 Stir in the black pepper and hot pepper sauce, and add salt. Serve hot.

EXTRA POINTS To prep this dish a day or two ahead, put the cooked bacon or sausage on a cookie sheet and place in the freezer for 15 to 30 minutes, then transfer it to a zipper-top plastic bag and freeze. Cook the scrambled eggs and let cool, place in another zipper-top plastic bag, and freeze. When ready to make the gruel, thaw the frozen bacon or sausage and eggs using the stove of your RV or a very hot grill and proceed with the recipe.

Shelley's Girly Breakfast Casserole

Shelley Kramer, a stylist at the salon where Anthony Nance keeps my hair looking winner's-circle good, says this brunch favorite appeals to women because it contains *vegetables* and chicken instead of the customary bacon and sausage. But sports-loving men like it, too. You can use frozen asparagus here, but it takes no time to lightly steam fresh asparagus, which will taste better. SERVES 10

8 slices potato bread
3/4 cup (1 1/2 sticks) butter, melted
2 cups shredded Mexican-blend cheese or
   cheddar cheese
2 cups chopped cooked asparagus

2 cups cubed cooked chicken
4 large eggs
2 cups milk (whole or low fat)
1 teaspoon salt
1 teaspoon freshly ground black pepper

1   Cut the bread into cubes and toss with the melted butter. In a buttered 9 x 13-inch baking dish, layer the ingredients in this order: half of the bread cubes, 1 cup of the cheese, 1 cup of the asparagus, all of the chicken, the remaining 1 cup asparagus, the remaining 1 cup cheese, and the remaining bread cubes.

2   In a large bowl, beat together the eggs, milk, salt, and pepper, and pour over the bread mixture. Cover with aluminum foil and refrigerate overnight.

3   Preheat the oven to 350°F.

4   Bake the casserole for 30 minutes, covered, then remove the aluminum foil and bake for another 30 to 45 minutes, or until the top is puffy and brown. Serve hot or warm.

EXTRA POINTS Note that you must refrigerate this overnight before baking. To speed baking, bring the casserole to room temperature before cooking.

Clota's Mountain Man Breakfast

Virginia Tech football fan Clota Gerhardt of Richmond, Virginia, says that this is a *hearty* dish for tailgating before a noon kickoff. It keeps Hokie fans stoked for the game. Clota originally got the recipe from an Internet site where Virginia Tech fans post their favorite recipes.   SERVES 12

1 pound bacon
2 medium-size onions, diced
1¹/₂ cups sliced white mushrooms
1 green bell pepper, diced
3 cloves garlic, minced
10 to 12 medium-size potatoes, peeled and
    sliced ¹/₂ inch thick

Salt and freshly ground black pepper to taste
1 dozen large eggs, beaten
3 cups shredded cheddar cheese
Bottled picante sauce for garnish

1   Heat a large, cast-iron Dutch oven over medium-high heat until very hot. Cut the bacon into 1-inch pieces and fry until brown. Add the onions, mushrooms, green pepper, and garlic, and sauté until the onions are translucent, about 5 minutes. Add the potatoes and season with salt and pepper. Lower the heat to medium, cover, and cook for 30 minutes.

2   Pour the beaten eggs over the mixture. Cover and cook for 20 minutes, or until the eggs are cooked and set.

3   Remove from the heat, sprinkle the cheese over the top, cover, and let stand until the cheese melts. Serve hot, topped with picante sauce.

EXTRA POINTS You can prepare the recipe the night before the tailgate, up to the point of adding the eggs in step 2. Put the mixture in an airtight container and refrigerate. For finishing at the tailgate, add the eggs and cook in the Dutch oven, covered, on a hot grill or burner.

Desserts

Great athletes know they must have a good *finish to win*, and these recipes will make sure your tailgate takes the checkered flag. Take some blondies along to your next parking-lot party, salute the Olympics by arranging *truffles* in the shape of the Olympic rings, or pour your best Kentucky *bourbon* for a pie that honors the Derby. Don't call a time-out now—there's lots to go.

Queenly Strawberries	135	
Jo Ann's Baked Apples Stuffed with Raisins	136	
Kim's Key Lime Pie Squares	137	
Coconut-Toffee Blondies	138	
Secret Ingredient Brownies	140	
Speedy Chocolate Truffles	141	
Krispy Kreme Bread Pudding	142	
Jim's Bourbon-Pecan Pie	143	
Go for the Gold Pie	145	
Norma's Brownie Pudding Cake	146	

Queenly Strawberries

Strawberries and *Cream* are traditionally served throughout the two-week Wimbledon tennis tournament outside London. Try this Italian-inspired twist on the classic breakfast at Wimbledon while watching the finals in July. SERVES 6 TO 8

4 cups sliced fresh strawberries
2½ teaspoons balsamic vinegar, aged 10 years or longer

About 1 teaspoon fresh lemon zest
1 cup crème fraîche
1 teaspoon confectioners' sugar

1   Place the strawberries in a bowl (not a metal one that will react with the acid in the vinegar), sprinkle the balsamic vinegar over them, and toss gently. Sprinkle the lemon zest on top.

2   In a small bowl, combine the crème fraîche and confectioners' sugar.

3   Serve the strawberries in individual bowls and pass the sweetened crème fraîche on the side.

EXTRA POINTS This simple dish is best prepared just before serving, though you can let the strawberries mingle with the vinegar and lemon zest for an hour or two. I strongly recommend that you purchase aged balsamic vinegar for this, which has an almost syrupy texture and an underlying sweetness. It's expensive, but worth it.

Jo Ann's Baked Apples Stuffed with Raisins

Race Mama Jo Ann Hlavac contributed this dessert that sweetens the wait for the green flag to drop. It's a great way to cook dessert on the grill while you're enjoying the main course. A *melon baller* may be helpful for hollowing out the apples. SERVES 4

4 Granny Smith apples
1/2 cup dark raisins

1/3 cup white or brown sugar
1 teaspoon ground cinnamon

1 Prepare a medium-hot fire in a charcoal grill.

2 Remove the cores of the apples so that the apples remain intact with a tube-like hole; do not go all the way through to the bottom of the apples.

3 Combine the raisins, sugar, and cinnamon in a small bowl. Stuff the mixture into the cored apples, pressing the filling down well. Wrap each apple separately in aluminum foil.

4 Place the apples in the embers of the charcoal fire and cook for 8 to 10 minutes, or until the apples are soft. Serve warm.

EXTRA POINTS **If you like, you may mix the filling before you head out, carrying it along in a zipper-top plastic bag. Then core, stuff, and cook the apples at the tailgate.**

Kim's Key Lime Pie Squares

Kim Hughes of Wake Forest, North Carolina, takes this *easy* dessert to feed hungry players, including her son, after soccer matches at the University of North Carolina at Chapel Hill.

SERVES 8 TO 12

1¹/₂ cups graham cracker crumbs
6 tablespoons (³/₄ stick) unsalted butter, melted
¹/₄ cup sugar

6 egg yolks
Two 14-ounce cans condensed milk
1 cup bottled Key lime juice

1   Preheat the oven to 350°F.

2   Combine the graham cracker crumbs, melted butter, and sugar in a medium-size bowl. Press the mixture into the bottom of a 9 x 13-inch baking dish. Bake for 8 minutes, or until lightly browned. Set aside to cool.

3   In a large bowl, whisk together the egg yolks and condensed milk. Add the Key lime juice and continue to whisk well to combine. Pour the mixture into the graham cracker crust and bake for 25 to 30 minutes. The center should be jiggly but not runny, much like the consistency of cheesecake. Let cool completely on a cooling rack, then refrigerate. Cut into squares before serving.

EXTRA POINTS Bake these 1 day ahead of time and keep them chilled until ready to serve.

Coconut-Toffee Blondies

Blondies are brownies of a different color with a butterscotch-like flavor. These sweet bars are chunky with *nuts*, *coconut*, and *toffee chips*. I adapted this recipe from one in *The American Century Cookbook* (Clarkson Potter Publishers, 1997), by Jean Anderson. MAKES 16 BARS

¾ cup all-purpose flour
1 teaspoon baking powder
½ teaspoon salt
¼ cup (½ stick) unsalted butter
1 cup firmly packed light brown sugar

1 large egg
1½ teaspoons pure vanilla extract
⅔ cup chopped pecans
½ cup shredded unsweetened coconut
½ cup toffee baking chips

1 Preheat the oven to 350°F. Spray an 8 x 8-inch square baking pan with nonstick cooking spray.

2 Sift the flour, baking powder, and salt onto a plate and set aside. Place the butter in a large saucepan over low heat and melt gently. When the butter is melted, add the brown sugar, stirring until the sugar is dissolved. Remove the pan from the heat and let cool for 5 minutes, then whisk in the egg and vanilla extract. Stir in the flour mixture, then add the pecans, coconut, and toffee chips.

3 Spread the mixture into the prepared pan and bake for 30 to 35 minutes, or until lightly browned and the edges are pulling away slightly from the pan. Remove to a wire rack and let cool completely in the pan before slicing.

EXTRA POINTS **Make these goodies up to 2 days before the tailgate, and store them in an airtight container at room temperature.**

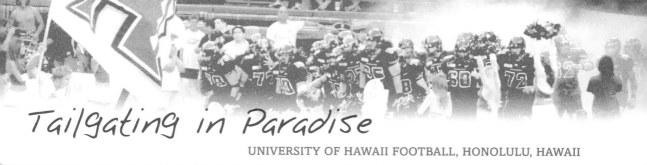

Tailgating in Paradise

UNIVERSITY OF HAWAII FOOTBALL, HONOLULU, HAWAII

*H*awaii is like nowhere else in the country, and tailgating there has its own flavor as well. Fans of the University of Hawaii Warriors don't feed on burgers and sausage, but on the abundance of seafood that comes from the waters around the islands. Honolulu food writer Jo McGarry, who does a pregame radio show during football season, says that hibachis rule in the parking lot, and that many tailgaters cook fish they caught themselves. "There's nothing quite like the taste of local fish, rubbed with some Hawaiian salt and seared on the grill," she says.

Mainland residents would be familiar with some of the seafood—*ahi* tuna, octopus, and *wahoo*, for example. But many fans grill up varieties of fish that are common to the islands, such as what Hawaiians call *aku*—skipjack tuna. It has a stronger fish flavor than the *ahi* tuna most people are familiar with from sushi bars. Besides grilling the fish, fans turn it into spreads or dips to snack on with slices of French bread. *Uku*, or gray snapper, is also popular.

Jo says that some fans do go elegant with tablecloths and silverware. But her favorite spots are where folks are talking about the game, popping beers, and waiting for a great meal to be ready. Some things are the same, after all, wherever you tailgate.

Secret Ingredient Brownies

Your fellow tailgaters will never guess what the subtle flavor is in these moist brownies, but they will notice how it seems to make the brownies taste more *chocolatey.* They'll keep your group talking—when they're not discussing game strategy, that is. **MAKES 24 BROWNIES**

5 ounces unsweetened chocolate
½ cup (1 stick) unsalted butter
1¼ cups all-purpose flour
½ teaspoon ground cinnamon
¾ teaspoon ground chile powder

3 large eggs
¾ cup granulated sugar
1 cup firmly packed light brown sugar
2 teaspoons pure vanilla extract
1 tablespoon vegetable oil

1 Preheat the oven to 350°F. Butter a 9 x 13-inch baking dish and set aside.

2 Place the chocolate and butter in a microwave-safe bowl and microwave on High for 2 minutes or until melted. Stir to combine the mixture, and set aside to cool until the bowl is only slightly warm to the touch, approximately 20 minutes. This mixture must be cooled or it will curdle the eggs.

3 Sift together the flour, cinnamon, and chile powder onto a plate and set aside. In a large bowl using an electric mixer, beat the eggs on medium speed until well mixed. Gradually stir in the granulated sugar, brown sugar, and vanilla extract, then beat on medium speed until the mixture is foamy. With the mixer on low, or by hand, gently stir the cooled chocolate mixture into the egg mixture. Stir in the flour mixture until well blended, then stir in the vegetable oil.

4 Pour the mixture into the prepared pan and bake for 25 minutes, or until a toothpick inserted in the center comes out clean. Remove to a wire rack and let cool completely in the pan before slicing.

EXTRA POINTS The brownies can be baked up to 2 days ahead of time and stored in an airtight container at room temperature.

Speedy Chocolate Truffles

These chocolate treats are quick, *bite-size*, and good.
I adapted them from a recipe I found in a cookbook produced
by the Women's Auxiliary of Motorsports, which supports
NASCAR drivers and charities.   MAKES ABOUT 40 TRUFFLES

One 11.5-ounce package bittersweet
   chocolate chips
1 teaspoon pure orange extract or
   1 1/2 teaspoons coffee-flavored liqueur

One 16-ounce can chocolate fudge icing
1/4 cup finely chopped pecans
Colored granulated sugars of your choice
About 40 small paper candy cups (optional)

1   Melt the chocolate chips in a bowl in the microwave on Low, being careful not to scorch the chocolate. Stir in the orange extract or coffee-flavored liqueur. Stir in the chocolate icing and the pecans and blend. Cover and refrigerate the mixture until cold and sticky, 30 to 45 minutes.

2   Remove the mixture from the refrigerator and shape by hand into approximately 1-inch balls. Roll the balls in colored sugar and place in paper candy cups if desired. Refrigerate until ready to serve.

EXTRA POINTS You can prepare these truffles several days ahead, refrigerating them in an airtight container in layers separated by waxed paper. Make sure to keep them chilled on the way to the tailgate. Use colored sugars (found in the baking or cake decorating sections of supermarkets) that match your favorite team or driver. You can also use finely chopped nuts or shredded coconut (tint it with food coloring, if you like) instead of sugar.

Krispy Kreme Bread Pudding

North Carolina's best-loved export (besides NASCAR racing) is Krispy Kreme *doughnuts*. This recipe is my combination of a basic bread pudding recipe and a Krispy Kreme version from *Hungry for Home* (Novello Festival Press, 2003), edited by Amy Rogers. I guarantee it will have your guests talking, no matter how fierce the action on the tube. SERVES 6 TO 8

10 day-old Krispy Kreme plain glazed doughnuts
3 large eggs
¹/₂ cup sugar

3 cups whole or 2 percent milk
1 teaspoon ground cinnamon
¹/₂ teaspoon ground nutmeg

1 Cut or tear the doughnuts into approximately 1-inch cubes. Spread the cubes evenly in the bottom of a 9 x 13-inch baking dish.

2 In a large bowl, whisk together the eggs, sugar, milk, cinnamon, and nutmeg until the sugar is dissolved. Pour the mixture over the doughnuts. Press gently with a spoon to be sure all the pieces are covered with liquid. Let stand at room temperature for 1 hour.

3 Preheat the oven to 350°F.

4 Bake the bread pudding for 1 hour and 30 minutes, or until the center is firm and cooked through. Cover with aluminum foil near the end of the baking time if the top is becoming too brown. Serve warm or at room temperature.

EXTRA POINTS This dish is best prepared shortly before serving.

Jim's Bourbon-Pecan Pie

The name "Derby Pie" is copyrighted by the Louisville, Kentucky, inn that claims to have invented the dessert. By any name, these *rich* pies are on the tables of fans everywhere when the first Saturday in May arrives. My food-loving friend Jim Crabtree of Raleigh, North Carolina, says he adapted this recipe from one from the Food Network. Jim uses frozen prepared pie crusts with excellent results.   MAKES ONE 9-INCH PIE

1 prepared refrigerated 9-inch pie crust
$^1/_4$ cup ($^1/_2$ stick) unsalted butter
2 ounces semisweet chocolate
3 large eggs
1 cup sugar

$^3/_4$ cup dark corn syrup
$^1/_2$ teaspoon pure vanilla extract
$^1/_3$ cup bourbon
$^1/_4$ teaspoon salt
$1^3/_4$ cups pecan halves

1   Preheat the oven to 350°F. Place the crust in a 9-inch pie pan.

2   Melt the butter and the chocolate in a small saucepan over medium-low heat. Remove the pan from the heat and let cool.

3   In a large mixing bowl, beat the eggs until frothy, then blend in the sugar. Stir in the corn syrup, vanilla extract, bourbon, salt, and the chocolate-butter mixture. Stir until well blended.

4   Place the pie pan on a cookie sheet. Spread the pecans evenly on the bottom of the pie crust, then carefully pour the filling mixture over them. Bake until the filling is set and slightly puffed, about 45 minutes. The pie is done when a thin knife inserted in the center comes out clean. Transfer the pie to a rack and let cool completely before cutting.

⭐ *EXTRA POINTS* You can prepare the pie the night before your tailgate and keep it chilled until ready to serve.

Spirit with a Heart

A bunch of Baltimore Ravens fans looked around one day and decided they had a choice. "We could drink beer and go to the football games, or we could drink beer, go to the games, and maybe raise a little money for charity," says Craig Reynolds. Fortunately for the Baltimore area, the group chose the second idea. Craig and other members of the Poe's Crows Club have raised about $60,000 for charity in the past eight years. The money has gone to a wide range of good causes, from a center for abused and neglected children to a former Baltimore football player who was suffering from a serious illness.

How do the Poe's Crows raise all that cash? Simply by doing what football fans do: tailgating. For each home game at the 70,000-seat M&T Bank Stadium, club members volunteer to prepare food at home or to man a custom-built grill and serve such things as burgers, bratwurst, and pit-cooked beef. The club sets up an all-you-can-eat tailgate buffet that's open to the public for $10 a head, and it typically serves 150 to 200 people a game.

Members, who pay annual dues, volunteer their time but are reimbursed for tailgate expenses. Information and menus are posted on the club's Web site, www.poescrows.com.

The Poe's Crows got started in 1996. The club name (and the football team name) refers to author Edgar Allan Poe, who lived in Baltimore. One can only imagine what the nineteenth-century poet and master of the macabre would think about the three Ravens mascots bearing his name cutting up at professional football games.

The Poe's Crows conduct other fundraising activities year round, but the tailgates are the club's centerpiece. The group often creates menus themed to the Ravens' opponents, such as a clambake and fish fry for the New England Patriots games. A few years ago, crawfish and alligator meat were shipped from Louisiana for a New Orleans Saints game.

Tailgating always is a time for great food and good friends, but the Poe's Crows have added an opportunity to be generous to those who need help. No matter what happens on the field, these Ravens fans are winners.

Go for the Gold Pie

A friend here in Raleigh, North Carolina, has a party each time the *Olympics* begin, with food inspired by the host country. For the 2006 Winter Olympics in Turin, Italy, I wanted to contribute a dessert that reflected the flavors of the region. Turin is famous for its chocolate-hazelnut candies, so I experimented with *Nutella* in this creamy, no-bake dessert. All the guests gave it a gold medal! Nutella is a chocolate-hazelnut spread; look for it in the peanut butter section of larger supermarkets or in specialty food stores. **SERVES 8**

One 8-ounce package cream cheese, softened
3/4 cup Nutella
1 teaspoon pure vanilla extract
1/3 cup sugar

1 cup cold heavy cream
1 prepared 9-inch graham cracker pie crust
Chopped toasted hazelnuts for garnish
Whipped cream for serving (optional)

1   In a large bowl using an electric mixer, combine the cream cheese, Nutella, vanilla extract, and sugar. Beat on medium speed until well blended. Set aside.

2   In a clean bowl with clean beaters or a balloon whisk, beat the heavy cream on medium-high until it holds soft peaks.

3   Scoop half of the whipped cream into the Nutella mixture and stir to blend. Add the rest of the whipped cream, folding it in gently.

4   Spoon the mixture into the pie crust and refrigerate for at least 4 hours. Before serving, sprinkle on the chopped toasted hazelnuts. Offer whipped cream on the side when serving, if desired.

EXTRA POINTS If you like, prepare the pie a day ahead and keep it chilled until serving time. For double chocolate flavor, substitute a prepared chocolate cookie pie crust for the graham cracker crust.

Norma's Brownie Pudding Cake

Chocolate is the fuel of sports fans everywhere, and the Iditarod sled dog race in Alaska is no exception. Norma Delia, one of the Skwentna Sweeties who feed mushers and volunteers, says this is a sweet dessert, "but they love it and we keep doing it." When adapting this recipe, I used dark, Dutch-processed *Cocoa Powder*, which gives the cake a rich flavor and deep color. SERVES 8

1¼ cups all-purpose flour
2 teaspoons baking powder
½ teaspoon salt
1½ cups granulated sugar
½ cup Dutch-processed cocoa powder
¾ cup milk

3 tablespoons unsalted butter, melted
1½ teaspoons pure vanilla extract
1 cup semisweet chocolate chips
1¾ cups boiling water
1 tablespoon confectioners' sugar

1   Preheat the oven to 350°F.

2   In a large bowl, combine the flour, baking powder, salt, ¾ cup of the granulated sugar, and ¼ cup of the cocoa powder. Add the milk, melted butter, and ¼ plus ⅛ teaspoon of the vanilla extract. Stir until smooth. Stir in the chocolate chips. Spread the mixture evenly on the bottom of an ungreased 9 x 13-inch baking dish.

3   In a medium-size bowl, whisk together the remaining ¾ cup granulated sugar and ¼ cup cocoa powder. Gradually stir in the boiling water and the remaining 1⅛ teaspoons vanilla extract. Carefully pour the mixture evenly over the batter in the baking dish.

4   Bake for 30 to 35 minutes, until the center is set and solid but not dry. Cool for 15 minutes. Sprinkle with the confectioners' sugar. Serve warm.

EXTRA POINTS You can make this cake up to 1 day ahead, but it will not have the same pudding texture in the middle when you cut it. If that's the result you'd like, bake this shortly before serving.

GAME PLANS

Menus for Every Occasion

NEW YEAR'S DAY FOOTBALL FEAST

Stout beer
Sweet-Hot Nuts   21
Alissa's Eight-Layer Dip   17
Lucy's Stout Steak Chili   62
Corny Cornbread   122
Mo's Mother's Coleslaw   110
Krispy Kreme Bread Pudding   142

SUPER BOWL OF SUPER BOWLS

Assorted beers
Foy's Patriot Clam Chowder   50
Don't Tell Them It's Good for Them
Vegetable Soup   47
Marvelous Mole Chili   64
Tossed salad and crusty bread
Norma's Brownie Pudding Cake   146

THE DAYTONA 500 GREAT AMERICAN FEED

Assortment of American microbrews
Revved-Up Onion Dip   16
served with chips and raw vegetables
Rub 'Em Out Wings   76
Quick Bean Medley for a Crowd   55
Bobbi's Spicy Slaw   112
Speedy Chocolate Truffles   141

ACC TOURNAMENT BRUNCH

Eddie's Bloody Mary   40
or Blue Lagoon   38
Slam-Dunk Sausage Balls   30
Big Game, Little Quiches   130
Teriyaki Tip-Off Wings   80
Martha's Seven-Layer Salad   108
Coconut-Toffee Blondies   138

KENTUCKY DERBY DELIGHT

Mint Juleps   36
or Brookhill Iced Tea   33
Rachel and Opal's Cheese Straws   19
Steeplechase Spread   14
Cool Classic Chicken Salad   119
Fresh Cucumber Salad   113
Jim's Bourbon-Pecan Pie   143

BREAKFAST AT WIMBLEDON

Denise's Mimosas   39
or English Breakfast tea
Rosemary-Garlic Pecans   20
Shelley's Girly Breakfast Casserole   132
Scones with jam and clotted cream
Queenly Strawberries   135

THRILLING GRILLING

Lynchburg Lemonade   35
Jo Ann's Foiled Chicken Poppers   22
Sizzling Citrus Grilled Steak   89
Kenny's Badadas   114
Kevin's Racin' Ears   116
Jo Ann's Baked Apples Stuffed
with Raisins   136

FANNING THE FLAMES

Satan's Whiskers   32
Marylynn's Okra Roll-Ups   27
Jo Ann's Campfire Onion Blossoms   29
Thomas's Marinated Gamecocks
with Polenta   86
Secret Ingredient Brownies   140

TAILGATING, SOUTHERN STYLE

Good Southern bourbon with your
favorite mixer or a big jug of iced tea
(sweet, of course)
Masterful PC, Southern Style   15
Cousin Judy's Deviled Eggs   125
Better-than-the-Bucket Fried Chicken   72
Mo's Mother's Coleslaw   110
Bread and butter pickles, watermelon rind
pickles, and pickled okra
Jim's Bourbon-Pecan Pie   143

A TAILGATE THANKSGIVING

California Chardonnay or Pinot Noir
Number One Sweet Potato Soup   46
Crowd-Pleasing
Marinated Green Beans   109
"Punkin" Mini-Muffins   123
Fast Lane Fried Turkey   82
Go for the Gold Pie   145

Measurement Equivalents

Please note that all conversions are approximate.

Liquid Conversions

U.S.	METRIC
1 tsp	5 ml
1 tbs	15 ml
2 tbs	30 ml
3 tbs	45 ml
$1/4$ cup	60 ml
$1/3$ cup	75 ml
$1/3$ cup + 1 tbs	90 ml
$1/3$ cup + 2 tbs	100 ml
$1/2$ cup	120 ml
$2/3$ cup	150 ml
$3/4$ cup	180 ml
$3/4$ cup + 2 tbs	200 ml
1 cup	240 ml
1 cup + 2 tbs	275 ml
$1^{1}/4$ cups	300 ml
$1^{1}/3$ cups	325 ml
$1^{1}/2$ cups	350 ml
$1^{2}/3$ cups	375 ml
$1^{3}/4$ cups	400 ml
$1^{3}/4$ cups + 2 tbs	450 ml
2 cups (1 pint)	475 ml
$2^{1}/2$ cups	600 ml
3 cups	720 ml
4 cups (1 quart)	945 ml (1,000 ml is 1 liter)

Oven Temperature Conversions

°F	GAS MARK	°C
250	$1/2$	120
275	1	140
300	2	150
325	3	165
350	4	180
375	5	190
400	6	200
425	7	220
450	8	230
475	9	240
500	10	260
550	Broil	290

Weight Conversions

U.S./U.K.	METRIC
$1/2$ oz	14 g
1 oz	28 g
$1^{1}/2$ oz	43 g
2 oz	57 g
$2^{1}/2$ oz	71 g
3 oz	85 g
$3^{1}/2$ oz	100 g
4 oz	113 g
5 oz	142 g
6 oz	170 g
7 oz	200 g
8 oz	227 g
9 oz	255 g
10 oz	284 g
11 oz	312 g
12 oz	340 g
13 oz	368 g
14 oz	400 g
15 oz	425 g
1 lb	454 g

Index

A

Alcohol and tailgating, note about, 7

Alissa's Eight-Layer Dip, 17

Aluminum foil, 3

Appetizers and snacks

Alissa's Eight-Layer Dip, 17

Big Game, Little Quiches, 130

Chip Shots, 18

Cousin Judy's Deviled Eggs, 125

Goal-to-Go Guacamole, 12

Gobble 'Em Up Nachos, 23

Jo Ann's Campfire Onion Blossoms, 29

Jo Ann's Foiled Chicken Poppers, 22

Lisa's Amazing Appetizer, 24

Marylynn's Okra Roll-Ups, 27

Masterful PC, Southern Style, 15

Munchable Marinated Shrimp, 28

Rachel and Opal's Cheese Straws, 19

Revved-Up Onion Dip, 16

Rosemary-Garlic Pecans, 20

Slam-Dunk Sausage Balls, 30

Smoky Quesadillas, 25

Steeplechase Spread, 14

Summer Tomato Spread, 13

Sweet-Hot Nuts, 21

Apples, Baked, Stuffed with Raisins, Jo Ann's, 136

Asparagus

Shelley's Girly Breakfast Casserole, 132

Avocados

Alissa's Eight-Layer Dip, 17

Goal-to-Go Guacamole, 12

Steeplechase Spread, 14

B

Bacon

Clota's Mountain Man Breakfast, 133

Jo Ann's Foiled Chicken Poppers, 22

Jo Ann's Rockingham Gruel, 131

Martha's Seven-Layer Salad, 108

BBQ Queens' Love Potion for the Swine, 95

Bean(s)

Alissa's Eight-Layer Dip, 17

Baked, New Year's Day, 54

Black, and Corn Soup, 48

Green, Marinated Crowd-Pleasing, 109

Lucy's Stout Steak Chili, 62–63

Medley, Quick, for a Crowd, 55

Red, and Rice, Party Time, 56–57

Smokin' Chicken Chili, 66

Smoky Quesadillas, 25

Very Veggie Lentil Chili, 60

Beef

Double Play Spicy, 88

Grilled Steak and Vegetable Skewers with Chimichurri Sauce, 90

internal temperatures for, 7

Beef *(continued)*

    Linda's Super Sauerkraut Stew, 96–97

    Lucy's Stout Steak Chili, 62–63

    Marvelous Mole Chili, 64–65

    Sizzling Citrus Grilled Steak, 89

Better-than-the-Bucket Fried Chicken, 72–73

Big Feed Jambalaya, 58–59

Big Game, Little Quiches, 130

Biscuits, Sweet Potato Ham, 120–21

Black Bean and Corn Soup, 48

Black-eyed peas

    Sheri's Carolina Caviar, 117

Blondies, Coconut-Toffee, 138

Bloody Mary, Eddie's, 40

Blue Lagoon, 38

Bobbi's Spicy Slaw, 112

Bottle openers, 3

Bourbon

    mint juleps, preparing, 36–37

    -Pecan Pie, Jim's, 143

Bread Pudding, Krispy Kreme, 142

Breads

    Chip Shots, 18

    Corny Cornbread, 122

    Elizabeth's Baked Hush Puppies, 124

    "Punkin" Mini-Muffins, 123

    Sweet Potato Ham Biscuits, 120–21

Breakfast and brunch

    Big Game, Little Quiches, 130

    Clota's Mountain Man Breakfast, 133

    Jo Ann's Rockingham Gruel, 131

    Michael's Sweet Potato Waffles, 126–27

    Shelley's Girly Breakfast Casserole, 132

Brookhill Iced Tea, 33

Brownie Pudding Cake, Norma's, 146

Brownies, Secret Ingredient, 140

Burgers

    cooking temperature, 7

    preparing patties ahead, 2

C

Cabbage

    Bobbi's Spicy Slaw, 112

    Don't Tell Them It's Good for Them Vegetable

        Soup, 47

    Linda's Super Sauerkraut Stew, 96–97

    Mo's Mother's Coleslaw, 110

    Sheri's Chinese Salad, 111

Cajun Seasoning, Salt-Free, 57

Cake, Brownie Pudding, Norma's, 146

Can openers, 3

Carrots

    Don't Tell Them It's Good for Them Vegetable

        Soup, 47

    Norma's Cool Veggie Pizza, 104

Casserole, Breakfast, Shelley's Girly, 132

Chairs, folding, 4

Charcoal, hardwood, 4, 5

Charcoal chimney starter, 4, 5

Cheddar cheese

    Alissa's Eight-Layer Dip, 17

    Clota's Mountain Man Breakfast, 133

    Gobble 'Em Up Nachos, 23

    Kim's PBF Chicken Enchiladas, 75

    Masterful PC, Southern Style, 15

    Rachel and Opal's Cheese Straws, 19

    Shelley's Girly Breakfast Casserole, 132

    Slam-Dunk Sausage Balls, 30

Cheese. *See also* Cream cheese

    Alissa's Eight-Layer Dip, 17

    Blue, Ball, Nutty, 26

Clota's Mountain Man Breakfast, 133

Double Play Spicy Beef, 88

Gobble 'Em Up Nachos, 23

Kim's PBF Chicken Enchiladas, 75

Lisa's Amazing Appetizer, 24

Masterful PC, Southern Style, 15

Shelley's Girly Breakfast Casserole, 132

Slam-Dunk Sausage Balls, 30

Smoky Quesadillas, 25

Straws, Rachel and Opal's, 19

Chicken

    Big Feed Jambalaya, 58–59

    Chili, Smokin', 66

    Dynamite Wings, 81

    Enchiladas, Kim's PBF, 75

    Fried, Better-than-the-Bucket, 72–73

    internal temperatures for, 7

    John's Corn Chowder, 53

    New Year's Day Slow Cooker Wings, 77

    Poppers, Foiled, Jo Ann's, 22

    Rub 'Em Out Wings, 76

    Salad, Cool Classic, 119

    with Sauce, Wally's Game, 70

    Shelley's Girly Breakfast Casserole, 132

    Tandoori Touchdown Wings with Mint-Mango
        Chutney, 78

    Teriyaki Tip-Off Wings, 80

    Tropical Herb, 74

Chiles

    Black Bean and Corn Soup, 48

    Bobbi's Spicy Slaw, 112

    Chipotle Dipping Sauce, 93

    chipotle puree, preparing, 42

    Dynamite Wings, 81

    Goal-to-Go Guacamole, 12

    Gobble 'Em Up Nachos, 23

Jo Ann's Foiled Chicken Poppers, 22

Kim's PBF Chicken Enchiladas, 75

Marvelous Mole Chili, 64–65

Red-Hot Cider, 43

Smokin' Chicken Chili, 66

Smokin' Mary, 42

Smoky Quesadillas, 25

Chili

    Lentil, Very Veggie, 60

    Marvelous Mole, 64–65

    Smokin' Chicken, 66

    Stout Steak, Lucy's, 62–63

Chimichurri Sauce, 91

Chipotle

    Dipping Sauce, 93

    puree, preparing, 42

Chip Shots, 18

Chocolate

    Go for the Gold Pie, 145

    Jim's Bourbon-Pecan Pie, 143

    Norma's Brownie Pudding Cake, 146

    Secret Ingredient Brownies, 140

    Truffles, Speedy, 141

Chowder

    Clam, Foy's Patriot, 50–51

    Corn, John's, 53

Chutney, Mint-Mango, 79

Cider, Red-Hot, 43

Cilantro-Peanut Dipping Sauce, 93

Clam(s)

    Chowder, Foy's Patriot, 50–51

    Jo's Hibachi Seafood Mix, 99

Clota's Mountain Man Breakfast, 133

Cocktails

    Blue Lagoon, 38

    Denise's Mimosas, 39

Cocktails (continued)
  Eddie's Bloody Mary, 40
  Lynchburg Lemonade, 35
  mint juleps, preparing, 36–37
  Satan's Whiskers, 32
  Smokin' Mary, 42
  Thomas's Tennessee, 31
  Whassup, Mary?, 41
Coconut-Toffee Blondies, 138
Cold foods, storing, 6
Coleslaw, Mo's Mother's, 110
Cool Classic Chicken Salad, 119
Coolers, 3, 7
Corkscrews, 3
Corn
  and Black Bean Soup, 48
  Carolina Champions Shrimp Bowl, 52
  Chowder, John's, 53
  Corny Cornbread, 122
  Kevin's Racin' Ears, 116
Cornbread, Corny, 122
Cornish game hens
  Thomas's Marinated Gamecocks with Polenta,
    86
Cornmeal
  Corny Cornbread, 122
  Elizabeth's Baked Hush Puppies, 124
  Polenta, 87
Couscous and Shrimp Salad, 102–3
Cousin Judy's Deviled Eggs, 125
Cream cheese
  Go for the Gold Pie, 145
  Lisa's Amazing Appetizer, 24
  Marylynn's Okra Roll-Ups, 27
  Norma's Cool Veggie Pizza, 104
  Nutty Blue Cheese Ball, 26

Crowd-Pleasing Marinated Green Beans, 109
Cucumber Salad, Fresh, 113
Cutting boards, 3, 6

D

Denise's Mimosas, 39
Desserts
  Coconut-Toffee Blondies, 138
  Go for the Gold Pie, 145
  Jim's Bourbon-Pecan Pie, 143
  Jo Ann's Baked Apples Stuffed with Raisins,
    136
  Kim's Key Lime Pie Squares, 137
  Krispy Kreme Bread Pudding, 142
  Norma's Brownie Pudding Cake, 146
  Queenly Strawberries, 135
  Secret Ingredient Brownies, 140
  Speedy Chocolate Truffles, 141
Deviled Eggs, Cousin Judy's, 125
Dinnerware, 3, 6
Dipping Sauce
  Chipotle, 93
  Cilantro-Peanut, 93
Dips and spreads
  Alissa's Eight-Layer Dip, 17
  chilling, before transporting, 6
  Goal-to-Go Guacamole, 12
  Masterful PC, Southern Style, 15
  Nutty Blue Cheese Ball, 26
  Revved-Up Onion Dip, 16
  Steeplechase Spread, 14
  Summer Tomato Spread, 13
Dishwashing liquid, 4
Disinfectant wipes, 4
Disposable gloves, 3, 6

Don't Tell Them It's Good for Them Vegetable
    Soup, 47
Double Play Spicy Beef, 88
Drinks
    Blue Lagoon, 38
    Brookhill Iced Tea, 33
    chilling, before transporting, 6
    Denise's Mimosas, 39
    Eddie's Bloody Mary, 40
    Homemade Limoncello, 34
    Lynchburg Lemonade, 35
    mint juleps, preparing, 36–37
    Red-Hot Cider, 43
    Satan's Whiskers, 32
    Smokin' Mary, 42
    Thomas's Tennessee Cocktail, 31
    Whassup, Mary?, 41
Dynamite Wings, 81

E

Eddie's Bloody Mary, 40
Eggs
    Clota's Mountain Man Breakfast, 133
    Deviled, Cousin Judy's, 125
    deviled, preparing ahead, 2
    Jo Ann's Rockingham Gruel, 131
    raw, safety issues, 6
Elizabeth's Baked Hush Puppies, 124
Enchiladas, Chicken, Kim's PBF, 75

F

Fast Lane Fried Turkey, 82–83
First-aid kit, 4
Fish
    Jo's Hibachi Seafood Mix, 99

Poached Salmon with Garlic-Yogurt Sauce,
    100–101
    testing for doneness, 7
Flashlights, 4
Foil pans, 3
Food safety considerations, 6–7
Foy's Patriot Clam Chowder, 50–51

G

Gamecocks, Marinated, with Polenta,
    Thomas's, 86
Gin
    Satan's Whiskers, 32
Ginger Scallops, Seared, Thomas's, 98
Gloves, disposable, 3, 6
Goal-to-Go Guacamole, 12
Gobble 'Em Up Nachos, 23
Go for the Gold Pie, 145
Green Beans, Crowd-Pleasing Marinated, 109
Grilled dishes
    Dynamite Wings, 81
    Grilled Pork Tenderloin with Dipping Sauces,
        92
    Grilled Steak and Vegetable Skewers with
        Chimichurri Sauce, 90
    Indoor/Outdoor Kiss-of-Fire-and-Smoke Ribs,
        94
    Jo Ann's Baked Apples Stuffed with Raisins,
        136
    Jo Ann's Campfire Onion Blossoms, 29
    Jo Ann's Foiled Chicken Poppers, 22
    Jo's Hibachi Seafood Mix, 99
    Kenny's Badadas, 114
    Kevin's Racin' Ears, 116
    Sizzling Citrus Grilled Steak, 89

Grilled dishes *(continued)*

    Tandoori Touchdown Wings with Mint-Mango
        Chutney, 78

    Thomas's Marinated Gamecocks with Polenta,
        86

    Tropical Herb Chicken, 74

    Wally's Game Chicken with Sauce, 70

Grilling supplies, 4

Grilling techniques, 5

Grits

    Jo Ann's Rockingham Gruel, 131

Guacamole, Goal-to-Go, 12

H

Ham

    Marylynn's Okra Roll-Ups, 27

    Sweet Potato Biscuits, 120–21

Hand sanitizer, 4, 6

Hickory Rub, Ole, 95

Homemade Limoncello, 34

Hush Puppies, Baked, Elizabeth's, 124

I

Ice, 3, 6

Iced Tea, Brookhill, 33

Indoor/Outdoor Kiss-of-Fire-and-Smoke Ribs,
    94

J

Jambalaya, Big Feed, 58–59

Jim's Bourbon-Pecan Pie, 143

Jo Ann's Baked Apples Stuffed with Raisins,
    136

Jo Ann's Campfire Onion Blossoms, 29

Jo Ann's Foiled Chicken Poppers, 22

Jo Ann's Rockingham Gruel, 131

Jo's Hibachi Seafood Mix, 99

K

Kenny's Badadas, 114

Kevin's Racin' Ears, 116

Key Lime Pie Squares, Kim's, 137

Kim's Key Lime Pie Squares, 137

Kim's PBF Chicken Enchiladas, 75

Knives, 3, 6

Krispy Kreme Bread Pudding, 142

L

Lanterns, battery-powered, 4

Lemons

    Blue Lagoon, 38

    Brookhill Iced Tea, 33

    Homemade Limoncello, 34

    Lynchburg Lemonade, 35

Lentil Chili, Very Veggie, 60

Lettuce

    Alissa's Eight-Layer Dip, 17

    Martha's Seven-Layer Salad, 108

Lighter fluid, 5

Lighter or matches, 4

Lime, Key, Pie Squares, Kim's, 137

Limoncello, Homemade, 34

Linda's Super Sauerkraut Stew, 96–97

Lobster

    Jo's Hibachi Seafood Mix, 99

Lucy's Stout Steak Chili, 62–63

Lynchburg Lemonade, 35

M

Main dishes

  Better-than-the-Bucket Fried Chicken, 72–73

  Big Feed Jambalaya, 58–59

  Cool Classic Chicken Salad, 119

  Double Play Spicy Beef, 88

  Dynamite Wings, 81

  Fast Lane Fried Turkey, 82–83

  Grilled Pork Tenderloin with Dipping Sauces, 92

  Grilled Steak and Vegetable Skewers with Chimichurri Sauce, 90

  Indoor/Outdoor Kiss-of-Fire-and-Smoke Ribs, 94

  Jo's Hibachi Seafood Mix, 99

  Kim's PBF Chicken Enchiladas, 75

  Linda's Super Sauerkraut Stew, 96–97

  Lucy's Stout Steak Chili, 62–63

  Marvelous Mole Chili, 64–65

  New Year's Day Slow Cooker Wings, 77

  Norma's Cool Veggie Pizza, 104

  Party Time Red Beans and Rice, 56–57

  Poached Salmon with Garlic-Yogurt Sauce, 100–101

  Rub 'Em Out Wings, 76

  Shrimp and Couscous Salad, 102–3

  Sizzling Citrus Grilled Steak, 89

  Smokin' Chicken Chili, 66

  Tandoori Touchdown Wings with Mint-Mango Chutney, 78

  Teriyaki Tip-Off Wings, 80

  Thomas's Marinated Gamecocks with Polenta, 86

  Thomas's Seared Ginger Scallops, 98

  Tropical Herb Chicken, 74

  Very Veggie Lentil Chili, 60

  Wally's Game Chicken with Sauce, 70

Mango-Mint Chutney, 79

Martha's Seven-Layer Salad, 108

Marvelous Mole Chili, 64–65

Marylynn's Okra Roll-Ups, 27

Masterful PC, Southern Style, 15

Mayonnaise, food safety and, 6

Meat. *See also* Beef; Pork

  raw, transporting, 6

Menus, 147–48

Michael's Sweet Potato Waffles, 126–27

Mimosas, Denise's, 39

Mint juleps, preparing, 36–37

Mint-Mango Chutney, 79

Mole Chili, Marvelous, 64–65

Mo's Mother's Coleslaw, 110

Muffins, Mini "Punkin," 123

Munchable Marinated Shrimp, 28

N

Nachos, Gobble 'Em Up, 23

New Year's Day Baked Beans, 54

New Year's Day Slow Cooker Wings, 77

Norma's Brownie Pudding Cake, 146

Norma's Cool Veggie Pizza, 104

Number One Sweet Potato Soup, 46

Nuts

  Coconut-Toffee Blondies, 138

  Cool Classic Chicken Salad, 119

  Jim's Bourbon-Pecan Pie, 143

  Nutty Blue Cheese Ball, 26

  Rosemary-Garlic Pecans, 20

  Sheri's Chinese Salad, 111

  Speedy Chocolate Truffles, 141

  Sweet-Hot, 21

O

Okra Roll-Ups, Marylynn's, 27
Olives
    Alissa's Eight-Layer Dip, 17
    Sheri's Carolina Caviar, 117
Onion
    Blossoms, Campfire, Jo Ann's, 29
    Dip, Revved-Up, 16
Oranges
    Denise's Mimosas, 39
    Satan's Whiskers, 32
    Sheri's Chinese Salad, 111
Oven mitts, 4

P

Paper towels, 4
Parrafin starter, 5
Party Time Red Beans and Rice,
    56–57
Peanut-Cilantro Dipping Sauce, 93
Peas
    Martha's Seven-Layer Salad, 108
    Polenta, 87
    Sheri's Carolina Caviar, 117
Pecan(s)
    -Bourbon Pie, Jim's, 143
    Coconut-Toffee Blondies, 138
    Cool Classic Chicken Salad, 119
    Rosemary-Garlic, 20
    Speedy Chocolate Truffles, 141
    Sweet-Hot Nuts, 21
Peppers. *See also* Chiles
    Gobble 'Em Up Nachos, 23
    Grilled Steak and Vegetable Skewers with
        Chimichurri Sauce, 90

Kenny's Badadas, 114
Martha's Seven-Layer Salad, 108
Masterful PC, Southern Style, 15
Mo's Mother's Coleslaw, 110
Norma's Cool Veggie Pizza, 104
Shrimp and Couscous Salad, 102–3
Pies
    Bourbon-Pecan, Jim's, 143
    Go for the Gold, 145
Pimientos
    Gobble 'Em Up Nachos, 23
    Masterful PC, Southern Style, 15
Pizza, Cool Veggie, Norma's, 104
Plastic bags, 3
Poached Salmon with Garlic-Yogurt Sauce,
    100–101
Polenta, 87
Pork. *See also* Bacon; Ham
    Big Feed Jambalaya, 58–59
    Indoor/Outdoor Kiss-of-Fire-and-Smoke Ribs,
        94
    internal temperatures for, 7
    Jo Ann's Rockingham Gruel, 131
    Linda's Super Sauerkraut Stew, 96–97
    Slam-Dunk Sausage Balls, 30
    Tenderloin, Grilled, with Dipping Sauces,
        92
Potato(es)
    Carolina Champions Shrimp Bowl, 52
    Clota's Mountain Man Breakfast, 133
    Don't Tell Them It's Good for Them Vegetable
        Soup, 47
    Foy's Patriot Clam Chowder, 50–51
    John's Corn Chowder, 53
    Kenny's Badadas, 114
    Sweet, Ham Biscuits, 120–21

Sweet, Soup, Number One, 46

Sweet, Waffles, Michael's, 126–27

Poultry. *See also* Chicken; Turkey

internal temperatures for, 7

Thomas's Marinated Gamecocks with Polenta, 86

Propane gas canister, 4

Pudding, Krispy Kreme Bread, 142

Pudding Cake, Brownie, Norma's, 146

"Punkin" Mini-Muffins, 123

Q

Queenly Strawberries, 135

Quesadillas, Smoky, 25

Quiches, Little, Big Game, 130

Quick Bean Medley for a Crowd, 55

R

Rachel and Opal's Cheese Straws, 19

Raisins, Jo Ann's Baked Apples Stuffed with, 136

Red-Hot Cider, 43

Revved-Up Onion Dip, 16

Rice

Big Feed Jambalaya, 58–59

Red Beans and, Party Time, 56–57

Rosemary-Garlic Pecans, 20

Rub 'Em Out Wings, 76

S

Salads

Bobbi's Spicy Slaw, 112

Chicken, Cool Classic, 119

chilling, before transporting, 6

Chinese, Sheri's, 111

Crowd-Pleasing Marinated Green Beans, 109

Cucumber, Fresh, 113

greens, washing and storing, 2

Mo's Mother's Coleslaw, 110

Seven-Layer, Martha's, 108

Sheri's Carolina Caviar, 117

Shrimp and Couscous, 102–3

Salmon, Poached, with Garlic-Yogurt Sauce, 100–101

Salt-Free Cajun Seasoning, 57

Satan's Whiskers, 32

Sauces

BBQ Queens' Love Potion for the Swine, 95

Chimichurri, 91

Dipping, Chipotle, 93

Dipping, Cilantro-Peanut, 93

Sauerkraut Stew, Linda's Super, 96–97

Sausage(s)

Balls, Slam-Dunk, 30

Big Feed Jambalaya, 58–59

Jo Ann's Rockingham Gruel, 131

Linda's Super Sauerkraut Stew, 96–97

Scallops

Jo's Hibachi Seafood Mix, 99

Seared Ginger, Thomas's, 98

Screwdriver, 4

Seafood

Carolina Champions Shrimp Bowl, 52

Foy's Patriot Clam Chowder, 50–51

Jo's Hibachi Seafood Mix, 99

Munchable Marinated Shrimp, 28

Poached Salmon with Garlic-Yogurt Sauce, 100–101

Seafood *(continued)*

    raw, transporting, 6

    Shrimp and Couscous Salad, 102–3

    testing for doneness, 7

    Thomas's Seared Ginger Scallops, 98

Seasoning mixes

    Ole Hickory Rub, 95

    Salt-Free Cajun Seasoning, 57

Secret Ingredient Brownies, 140

Shelley's Girly Breakfast Casserole, 132

Shellfish

    Carolina Champions Shrimp Bowl, 52

    Foy's Patriot Clam Chowder, 50–51

    Jo's Hibachi Seafood Mix, 99

    Munchable Marinated Shrimp, 28

    Shrimp and Couscous Salad, 102–3

    testing for doneness, 7

    Thomas's Seared Ginger Scallops, 98

Sheri's Carolina Caviar, 117

Sheri's Chinese Salad, 111

Shrimp

    Bowl, Carolina Champions, 52

    Carolina Champions Shrimp Bowl, 52

    and Couscous Salad, 102–3

    Jo's Hibachi Seafood Mix, 99

    Marinated, Munchable, 28

Side dishes

    Big Game, Little Quiches, 130

    Bobbi's Spicy Slaw, 112

    Corny Cornbread, 122

    Cousin Judy's Deviled Eggs, 125

    Crowd-Pleasing Marinated Green Beans, 109

    Elizabeth's Baked Hush Puppies, 124

    Fresh Cucumber Salad, 113

    Kenny's Badadas, 114

    Kevin's Racin' Ears, 116

Martha's Seven-Layer Salad, 108

Mo's Mother's Coleslaw, 110

New Year's Day Baked Beans, 54

Party Time Red Beans and Rice, 56–57

Polenta, 87

"Punkin" Mini-Muffins, 123

Quick Bean Medley for a Crowd, 55

Sheri's Carolina Caviar, 117

Sheri's Chinese Salad, 111

Sweet Potato Ham Biscuits, 120–21

Sizzling Citrus Grilled Steak, 89

Slam-Dunk Sausage Balls, 30

Slaws

    Bobbi's Spicy, 112

    Mo's Mother's Coleslaw, 110

Slow cooker dishes

    Lucy's Stout Steak Chili, 62–63

    New Year's Day Baked Beans, 54

    New Year's Day Slow Cooker Wings, 77

Smokin' Chicken Chili, 66

Smokin' Mary, 42

Smoky Quesadillas, 25

Soups. *See also* Chili; Stews

    Black Bean and Corn, 48

    Foy's Patriot Clam Chowder, 50–51

    John's Corn Chowder, 53

    Sweet Potato, Number One, 46

    Vegetable, Don't Tell Them It's Good for Them, 47

Spatulas, 4

Speedy Chocolate Truffles, 141

Spoons, serving, 3

Sporting events

    Baltimore Ravens Football, 144

    Brookhill Steeplechase, 128–29

    Carolina Hurricanes Hockey, 71

Green Bay Packers pro football, 118

Iditarod Trail Sled Dog Race, 105

Kentucky Derby, 36–37

Milwaukee Brewers Baseball, 61

NASCAR racing, 115

Ole Miss college football, 67

University of Hawaii football, 139

University of South Carolina football, 49

Squash

Grilled Steak and Vegetable Skewers with
Chimichurri Sauce, 90

Norma's Cool Veggie Pizza, 104

"Punkin" Mini-Muffins, 123

Steeplechase Spread, 14

Stews

Carolina Champions Shrimp Bowl, 52

Sauerkraut, Linda's Super, 96–97

Strawberries, Queenly, 135

Summer Tomato Spread, 13

Sweet-Hot Nuts, 21

Sweet Potato

Ham Biscuits, 120–21

Soup, Number One, 46

Waffles, Michael's, 126–27

T

Tablecloths, 3

Tables, folding, 4

Tailgate party planning, 1–8

alcoholic beverages, 7

food safety considerations, 6–7

grilling tips and techniques, 5

history of, 9

menus for every occasion, 147–48

monthly sporting events, 8

supplies checklist, 3–4

timesaving tips, 2

Tandoori Touchdown Wings with Mint-Mango
Chutney, 78

Tea, Iced, Brookhill, 33

Tennessee Cocktail, Thomas's, 31

Teriyaki Tip-Off Wings, 80

Thermometer, instant-read, 4

Thermoses, 3

Thomas's Marinated Gamecocks with Polenta,
86

Thomas's Seared Ginger Scallops, 98

Thomas's Tennessee Cocktail, 31

Toffee-Coconut Blondies, 138

Tomato(es)

Alissa's Eight-Layer Dip, 17

Don't Tell Them It's Good for Them Vegetable
Soup, 47

Eddie's Bloody Mary, 40

Norma's Cool Veggie Pizza, 104

Sheri's Carolina Caviar, 117

Smokin' Mary, 42

Spread, Summer, 13

Whassup, Mary?, 41

Tongs, 4

Tortillas

Gobble 'Em Up Nachos, 23

Kim's PBF Chicken Enchiladas, 75

Smoky Quesadillas, 25

Trash bags, 3

Tropical Herb Chicken, 74

Truffles, Speedy Chocolate, 141

Turkey

Fried, Fast Lane, 82–83

frying, safey considerations, 84–85

Gobble 'Em Up Nachos, 23

V

Vegetable(s). *See also specific vegetables*
    Martha's Seven-Layer Salad, 108
    Norma's Cool Veggie Pizza, 104
    Soup, Don't Tell Them It's Good for Them, 47
    and Steak Skewers, Grilled, with Chimichurri
        Sauce, 90
Vermouth
    Satan's Whiskers, 32
Very Veggie Lentil Chili, 60
Vinegar, herb-flavored, preparing, 109
Vodka
    Blue Lagoon, 38
    Eddie's Bloody Mary, 40
    Homemade Limoncello, 34
    Smokin' Mary, 42
    Whassup, Mary?, 41

W

Waffles, Sweet Potato, Michael's, 126–27
Wally's Game Chicken with Sauce, 70
Water, for cleanup use, 4, 6
Whassup, Mary?, 41
Whiskey
    Lynchburg Lemonade, 35
    Thomas's Tennessee Cocktail, 31
Wrench, 4

Y

Yogurt-Garlic Sauce, Poached Salmon with,
    100–101

TEXT PHOTOGRAPHY CREDITS

iii, 10: Photo of Notre Dame Stadium courtesy of University of Notre Dame Sports Information Office

vii, ix: © Wally Gobetz

xi, 73, 106, 107, 115, 151: Photos courtesy of the Bristol Motor Speedway

1: © Stephen Nowland/Rich Clarkson and Assoc.

9: © Eliza Snow

11, 35, 45 (serving soup), 59, 69, 121, 148: © Jamie Schwaberow/Rich Clarkson and Assoc.

12, 20, 32, 39, 45 (buffet line), 51, 79, 87, 91, 101: © Trevor Brown Jr./Rich Clarkson and Assoc.

31, 103: © Nathan Watkins

36–37: Photo of horse race courtesy of Kushal Mukherjee

44, 147: Photo of Michigan Wolverines and Boston Celtics courtesy of Abby Collier

49: Photo of Cockaboose courtesy of University of South Carolina Media Relations

61: Photo of Miller Park tailgate courtesy of Gloria Strehlow

63, 83, 127, 147: © Sean Locke

65, 97: © Bill Grove

67: © Jeff Sands

68, 118: © Jim Biever

71: Photo of Carolina Hurricanes courtesy of Gregg Forwerck

105: © Ken Babione

128–129: Photo of Brookhill Steeplechase courtesy of Jeff King

134: Photo of Carter-Finley Stadium courtesy of Gene Galin

139: © Kevin Mullet

144: Photo of Poe's Crows Club courtesy of Terry Kuta

Cover photographs © Joyce Oudkerk Pool